Justice for the Past

SUNY series in American Constitutionalism

Robert J. Spitzer, editor

Justice for the Past

Stephen Kershnar

State University of New York Press

Published by
State University of New York Press, Albany

Printed in the United States of America

For information, address State University of New York Press,
90 State Street, Suite 700, Albany, NY 12207

Production by Michael Haggett
Marketing by Anne M. Valentine

Library of Congress Cataloging-in-Publication Data

Kershnar, Stephen.
Justice for the past / Stephen Kershnar.
p. cm. — (SUNY series in American constitutionalism)
Includes bibliographical references and index.
ISBN 0-7914-6071-1 (hard : alk. paper) — ISBN 0-7914-6072-X (pbk. : alk. paper)
1. Minorities—Civil rights—United States. 2. Women's rights—United States. 3. Minorities—Government policy—United States. 4. Women—Government policy—United States. 5. Affirmative action programs—United States. 6. African Americans—Reparations. I. Title. II. Series.

JC599.U5K447 2004
323.173—dc22

2004045254

10 9 8 7 6 5 4 3 2 1

Dedicated to my father,
Larry Kershnar

Contents

Acknowledgments xi

SECTION 1

Introduction 3

SECTION 2
Civil Rights Laws

1 The Most Qualified Applicant 11
- Part 1. The Job Qualification 14
- Part 2. The Best Conception of a Job Qualification Yields at Most a Very Weak Reason to Favor a Meritocracy 22
- Part 3. Antidiscrimination Laws Cannot Be Justified by Meritocratic Concerns 26
- Part 4. Qualifications for Educational Institutions 27
- Part 5. Conclusion 30

SECTION 3
Strong Affirmative Action

2 Strong Affirmative-Action Programs at State Institutions 33
- Part 1. Introduction 33
- Part 2. The Duty to Judge Persons according to Their Interests and Desert 35
- Part 3. Strong Affirmative-Action Programs at State Educational Institutions Cannot Be Justified via Compensatory Justice 40
- Part 4. Conclusion 51

3 Uncertain Damages to Racial Minorities and Strong Affirmative Action 53

Part 1. The Hypothetical Imperative to Distribute Resources in a Just Manner 53
Part 2. Compensatory Justice and the Assessment of Damages 54
Part 3. Compensatory Justice and Inadequate Knowledge of Damages 55
Part 4. We Do Not Have Adequate Knowledge of the Amount of Compensable Injury to Current Members of Some Racial Minority Groups 58
Part 5. Conclusion 64

SECTION 4
Reparations for Slavery

4 The Inheritance-Based Claim to Reparations 69

Part 1. Introduction 70
Part 2. Slavery Did Not Harm the Descendants of Slaves 70
Part 3. Compensation May Be Owed to the Descendants of Slaves As a Result of a Legitimate Inheritance Claim 76
Part 4. Conclusion 81

5 Reject the Inheritance-Based Claim to Reparations 83

Part 1. Objections to the Inheritance-Based Claim to Reparations 83
Part 2. Who Owes Compensation? 87
Part 3. Conclusion 91

SECTION 5
Proper Respect

6 Intrinsic Moral Value and Racial Differences 95

Part 1. The Expression of Equal Moral Value 95
Part 2. The Argument 98
Part 3. Implications of the Argument 111
Part 4. Conclusion 115

SECTION 6
Educational Diversity

7 Experiential Diversity 119
Part 1. *Grutter* and *Bakke* 120
Part 2. Experiential Diversity and Truth 122
Part 3. A More General Approach to Diversity 126
Part 4. Equal-Opportunity Arguments 128
Part 5. Conclusion 129

Notes 131

Index 157

Acknowledgments

I am grateful to many persons who taught me to think for myself rather than to merely accept conventional thinking. My parents, Larry and Arlene Kershnar, showed me both through our many conversations and through their lives how to think for myself and scrutinize issues with honesty and disciplined analysis. As important, they showed me the emotional difficulty that independent thought requires and provided me with love so that I could develop the required emotional well-being and physical strength to engage in it. My brother and I often discuss the various issues; without these conversations, I never would have completed this book. It is a great feeling to be part of a team. Also, my extended family has always made me feel loved and special. This includes my grandparents (especially Philip Kutner), my aunts and uncles (e.g., Judy and Gus Rubin, Rose Maidoff, and Doris and Bob Baker), and my cousins (e.g., Arlene, Jon, and Amy). They helped make my childhood an enjoyable one. My family, especially Toni, makes life enjoyable.

I owe a great intellectual debt to Neil Feit, Louis P. Pojman, and Michael Levin. These men have rigorous analytical minds and a wonderful philosophical temperament. I have spent many an hour wondering how to respond to Neil's powerful objections and how to incorporate his insightful suggestions. The work of Mike and Louis has greatly shaped my thinking on numerous issues, and I am fortunate to be able to work with such important philosophers. I also have an enormous debt to the friends and colleagues who have shared their lives and philosophical thoughts with me. They include (in no particular order) Andrea Koppelman, Michael Tonderum, Paul Marvin, Eric Laumann, Aaron Krauss, Susan Vineberg, and Prasanta Bandyopadhyay. I also benefited tremendously from the advice and philosophical insight of Robert Audi and Lawrence Lombard. Their careful analytic style and generosity as persons made a big difference in my intellectual development.

This book contains material that has been or will be published, although with modifications and additions. Most of chapter 1 will appear as "The Duty to Hire the Most Qualified Applicant" in *The Journal of Social Philosophy*. Parts of chapter 2 appeared as "Strong Affirmative Action Programs at State

Educational Institutions Cannot Be Justified via Compensatory Justice" in *Public Affairs Quarterly* 11 (1997): 345–64 and as "Strong Affirmative Action and Disproportionate Burdens" in *The Journal of Value Inquiry* 33 (1999): 201–209. Chapter 3 appeared as "Uncertain Damages to Racial Minorities and Strong Affirmative Action" in *Public Affairs Quarterly* 13 (1999): 83–84. Part of chapter 4 appeared as "Are the Descendants of Slaves Owed Compensation for Slavery?" in *Journal of Applied Philosophy* 16 (1999): 95–101. Chapters 4 and 5 will appear as "The Inheritance-Based Claim to Reparations" in *Legal Theory*. Part of chapter 6 appeared as "Intrinsic Moral Value and Racial Differences" in *Public Affairs Quarterly* 14 (2000): 205–24. Part of chapter 7 will appear as "Experiential Diversity and Grutter" in *Public Affairs Quarterly*. I am grateful to the following persons for their extraordinarily helpful comments and criticisms of these chapters: James Allard, Robert Audi, Prasanta Bandyopadhyay, Raymond Belliotti, Nicholas Capaldi, Neil Feit, Michael Levin, Lawrence Lombard, Louis P. Pojman, Lawrence Powers, Bruce Russell, George Schedler, Michael Tonderum, and Dale Tuggy.

SECTION 1

Introduction

One of the most controversial political topics in the United States is whether there should be strong affirmative-action programs and reparations for slavery. Much less controversial are the antidiscrimination provisions that constitute the civil rights laws. All three of these are often argued for on the basis of the value of compensating African Americans and to a lesser extent other minority groups and women for past injustices. In this book I explore these arguments.

Strong affirmative-action programs are ones that give preference to minority and women candidates who are less qualified than other applicants, with regard to a job, an educational opportunity, or some other benefit, for a limited range of reasons. The reasons cited are either backward-looking (i.e., justified by past events) or forward-looking (i.e., justified by future outcomes). The foremost backward-looking reason is compensatory justice. Compensatory justice involves the injured party's claim to compensation for an unjust harm. Employers and other institutions also have a number of what appear to be forward-looking reasons to institute strong affirmative-action programs. They often cite the goal of diversity. The last goal is usually a means by which to provide historically oppressed minority groups benefits such as role models, mentors, or a sufficient number of members so that group members do not feel isolated or that they are mere tokens. Also, promoting racial or sexual diversity is sometimes a way in which an institution or employer attempts to broaden the range of viewpoints that are present. In addition, diversity can be a means by which an employer promotes equal opportunity. Upon examination, the backward- and forward-looking motivations often tend to be either an attempt to identify the most qualified applicant or to provide just compensation for historically oppressed groups. For example, a unique perspective is in some contexts an important qualification rather than an attempt to promote members of historically disadvantaged groups. However, in cases in which the attempt is not aimed at satisfying a job qualification but another goal (e.g., equal opportunity or the presence of role models), then the underlying motivation is often compensatory. This is because the notion that steps should be taken to provide role models or equal opportunity often rests on the idea that such treatment is a permissible, if not required, response to past injustices. In exploring these issues, the first step is to determine what a job (or an educational) qualification is so that cases of strong affirmative action can then be more readily identified.

In chapter 1 I conclude that the most qualified job applicant is the one who has the propensity to maximally satisfy the employer's preferences. I fill out this applicant's propensity in terms of his willingness to work hard together with the relevant capacity or potentiality to do the tasks constituting a job. I then note that an analogous account can be given with regard to the most qualified applicant to an educational or other institution. Given this account of the most qualified applicant, I argue that there is only a weak duty, if any, to hire persons on the basis of their being the most qualified. Such a duty is not justified by reference to rights, desert, fairness, or the maximization of welfare. However, such a duty may come about via promises made by the employer or his agents. These results suggest that antidiscrimination laws cannot be justified on the basis of merit, although other justifications might still be available. Having provided an analysis of a job (and an educational) qualification, we are then in a position to explore whether it is morally permissible for the state and private entities to choose lesser-qualified persons via strong affirmative-action programs. I do this in chapters 2 and 3.

In chapter 2 I explore strong affirmative action at state institutions. In both state and private educational institutions, there are stark differences in the entrance standards for various racial and ethnic groups. A few examples of these differences include:

- The University of Texas Law School used an overall score for applicants that incorporated college grades and test scores. The median index score for blacks was lower than the lowest index with which any single white student was admitted, and only two white students were admitted with an index as low as the median index among Mexican Americans.[1]
- In a study of U.S. elite colleges and universities for 1991 and 1992, the difference in the sum of the average Verbal and Math SAT averaged 180 points (about 1.3 standard deviations), reaching as high as 288 points at the University of California at Berkeley.[2] The SAT is a better predictor of academic success at the university level than alternative measures (e.g., high school grades, interviews, and recommendations), and blacks' SAT scores slightly overpredict black performance.[3]
- At ten highly selective law schools for which individual data were reported in a 1977 report by the Law School Admissions Council, the average black-white difference in the standardized test (i.e., the LSAT) scores was 2.9 standard deviations, which is equivalent to saying that the average black was in the bottom 1 percent of the white distribution. In

studies of the LSAT differences in law schools in 1992, the difference between Latinos and whites was one standard deviation, and between whites and Puerto Ricans it was double that amount.[4]
- Results similar to those reported for law school scores are reported with regard to medical school scores.[5]

In the context of state programs, I argue that young white males are owed a duty to respect their interest and to give them what they deserve. This is because it is doubtful that persons would consent to a state that did not adopt policies that fairly weigh members' interests and desert, and because the state's authority rests on either consent or fairness. I then argue that not all white males have waived this duty, since many have not performed culpable wrongdoings toward members of historically oppressed groups. Nor, I argue, does merely having benefited from past injustices or being a member of a community that owes a debt of compensation to racial minorities and women constitute justify overriding the duty owed to the white male. I conclude that such programs probably cannot be justified by compensatory justice. I then note that this reasoning can be generalized to apply to state employment decisions.

In chapter 3, my conclusion is again that strong affirmative-action programs are not justified on the basis of compensatory justice. I begin by noting that unlike the state, private parties have the right to hire and give resources to whomever they want. However, they, as well as the state, would violate hypothetical imperatives if they implement such programs as the means by which to provide just compensation to historically oppressed groups. I argue that we should adopt the following principle with regard to compensatory justice: If an unjust act benefits an innocent person, and there is no reasonable way to assess the amount of the damages to the victim, then compensatory justice does not require that the innocent beneficiary pay compensation for those damages. I then argue that we cannot reasonably assess the amount of damages to current racial minorities resulting from past discriminatory acts. Problems arise in determining the identity of the injured parties, the identity of the injuring agents and injuring acts (and omissions), and the degree of injury that directly resulted from these acts (and omissions). Since such compensable damages cannot be accurately estimated, and since white male applicants are innocent beneficiaries of past discriminatory acts, the value of compensatory justice does not justify strong affirmative-action programs.

Having argued for the wrongfulness of state-sponsored, strong, affirmative-action programs, I then explore the case for reparations for slavery in chapters 4 and 5. A few instances of the movement for reparations[6] include:

- In 1994, according to the Internal Revenue Service, more than 20,000 African Americans refused to pay taxes (and indicated this refusal by writing "exempt" on the tax form) on the grounds that the money should go toward the descendants of slaves.[7]

- In 1989, Representative John Conyers of Michigan proposed legislation that would create a commission to explore the effects of slavery on both African Americans and the United States.
- One activist calculates that whites owe each black family $198,149, which is the value of forty acres and a mule at the time slavery was ended in 1865, plus the interest that would have accrued over the subsequent years.[8]
- Philosopher Bernard Boxill argues that the descendants of slaves are owed the compensation that should have been given to the slaves.[9]

The argument for reparations differs from the argument for strong affirmative-action programs, since the policies differ with regard to the distribution of the compensatory burdens and the relevant counterfactuals. In chapter 4 I argue that slavery harmed the slaves but not their descendants, since slavery brought about their existence. The descendants may, however, still own the slaves' claims via inheritance and thus are owed reparations. In chapter 5 I argue against this notion. I begin by noting that determining whether the inheritance-based claims still exist, and their amount, is extremely problematic. First, every descendant usually has no more than a portion of the slave's claim, because the claim is often divided over generations. Second, there are epistemic difficulties involving the ownership of the claim, since it is unlikely that a descendant of a slave several generations removed would have retained the claim of inheritance given the loss of wealth and disinheritance that often characterizes families. Third, there are problems in determining the amount of inheritance. This is in part because of the problems of calculating in the effects of offsets, especially crime-related offsets, which are owed by a significant portion of the descendants. When combined, these difficulties constitute an overwhelming case against reparations being owed by state or private parties.

In chapter 6 I explore whether the state's refusal to provide compensation constitutes a failure to condemn past injustices and thereby results in the state failing to express blacks' equal moral worth. My concern relates to the Kantian notion that at its core justice focuses on whether one's thoughts and actions express persons' equal moral worth. The underlying idea is that the Kantian imperative prohibits certain ways of thinking and acting toward persons (i.e., in degrading, unequal, and non-universalizable ways). These ways are not solely a function of persons' specific rights (e.g., rights to property). The value of such expression is understood in terms of its fittingness rather than its role in communication. On this account, the state might express contempt for black persons by failing to compensate them for past injustices. Such a failure may express the notion that blacks have less moral value than other persons. Treatment that expresses the notion that blacks have less value than other groups does not disrespect them as persons if they have, on average, less intrinsic value than other persons. In this chapter, I explore whether this is the case.

In this book, I argue that affirmative action and reparations are not justified on compensatory grounds. My project is somewhat disconnected from the real-world debate, especially the legal debate, which has focused in the academic context largely on the forward-looking grounds, especially educational diversity. This is explained by the purpose of this book, which is to investigate the backward-looking arguments for affirmative action and reparations. In chapter 7 I assess the dominant legal argument for affirmative action in colleges and universities and then relate it to the backward-looking arguments that are the focus of this book. I begin by observing that federal courts have split on whether preferential treatment was held to be constitutional on the basis of the contribution of "diverse" students to the education of their classmates. An implicit assumption in this argument is that the contribution involves making it more likely that the other students adopt the beliefs (or perspective) of the minorities. I argue that this argument is a weak one, since the beliefs are likely false, and in any case they are already well represented on campuses.

A point about methodology is also useful here. Philosophical arguments are useful as a way to bring out and evaluate the assumptions that are implicit in arguments for different policies. For example, one of the dominant arguments for affirmative action rests on the government's obligation to compensate current individuals for the evils of past discrimination and slavery. This presupposes theories of the nature of harm and government-owed compensation. These theories need to be recognized and evaluated, and my philosophical arguments, including the ones that rest on intuitions, are designed to do this. Philosophical investigations often use intuitions and analogies. This reflects the notion that coherence with intuitions and other plausible principles is often the only currently available method by which to adjudicate between competing theories. As a result, I make regular use of intuitions and analogies as ways to justify various conclusions about job qualifications, affirmative action, and reparations.

SECTION 2

Civil Rights Laws

1

The Most Qualified Applicant

Meritocracy is a system in which jobs or educational positions are given to the most qualified persons. Since the most qualified person may not be interested in serving in a particular job (or enrolling in a particular educational program), meritocracy in a society that has a healthy respect for liberty usually focuses on positions being given to the most qualified applicant. In this chapter, I argue that employers probably have no duty to hire the most qualified applicant. I focus on private employers to avoid the debate over the proper function of government entities. The discussion in this chapter of moral considerations surrounding the hiring of the most qualified applicant also sets up the discussion of strong affirmative action in the next two chapters, since this policy involves employers and other institutions selecting persons other than the most qualified applicant. Chapter 2 discusses where the state does this, and chapter 3 discusses where a private party does it.

My argument suggests that common intuitions with regard to merit and a common justification of the 1964 Civil Rights Act and other laws banning race and sex discrimination in the private realm cannot be sustained. For example, many people intuit that discrimination in favor of the most attractive model is appropriate for an advertising agency or in favor of the actress with large, shapely breasts is appropriate for a company making a movie about Las Vegas showgirls. They also view a college health center's choice of a female gynecologist as appropriate, where the largely female clientele have a strong preference for a female and are known to be much more likely to candidly discuss health issues with her than with a male gynecologist. In these cases, the nature of the job and the greater business efficacy of such persons combine to make these criteria seem acceptable. In contrast, many of these same people view the choice of a secretary or an air flight attendant in part on the basis of her physical attractiveness, or a bartender in part on the basis of his whiteness as unacceptable, even where such criteria reflect customer preference and increase profitability. These intuitions differ in content. Sometimes they involve the view that attractiveness or whiteness is not a job qualification, and sometimes they involve the view that these are job qualifications but that an employer ought not engage in strict qualification-based hiring.

In part 1 of this chapter, I argue that the most qualified job applicant is to be identified by reference to the employer's preferences. I proceed by initially exploring the concept of a job qualification and then argue for a particular conception that focuses on the value of autonomy. In part 2, I argue that given this account of a job qualification, there is probably no duty to hire the most qualified. In part 3, I argue that this case thus undermines the meritocratic justification for antidiscrimination laws. In part 4, I fill out the notion of the most qualified applicant to an educational institution. The notion of the most qualified applicant in employment and educational settings then sets up the discussion of strong affirmative action that occurs in the next two chapters.

The Civil Rights Act: An Opposing View

The position opposed to mine can be seen in the motivation for and interpretation of the 1964 Civil Rights Act. This act prevents race, sex, national origin, or religion from being used as a criterion for hiring. This act was defended in part on the basis that these attributes are not job qualifications and are thus unrelated to merit.[1] The act has an exception for cases in which these attributes are bona fide occupational qualifications (BFOQs), that is, qualifications that relate to a position's essential functions.[2] There is a BFOQ exception for race only where it involves authenticity or genuineness, for example, as it relates to actors and actresses.[3] The BFOQ case law (and the related case law on business necessity) sets out a number of reasons that will not support sex, national origin, or religion being BFOQs. In particular, a BFOQ cannot rest on business-related concerns such as profit loss and tort liability or on non-business concerns relating to safety of fetuses (and the persons they are or become) and in some cases the privacy of clientele.[4] More importantly, it rules out customer preferences where these preferences are unrelated to a job's essential function or where they rest on a stereotype.[5] In addition, the bona fide occupational qualification has been interpreted to require a business necessity test (or something approximating it).[6] This test sets an imposing standard because it is hard to show that a practice is necessary for a business to remain viable and because it is independent of what the employer knew or should have known of the appropriate standard. This narrow reading of the qualification rule both implicitly and at times explicitly involves the court's asserting that the essence of a job is not solely a function of the employer's preferences. Two cases illustrate this assertion.

In *Diaz v. Pan Am World Airways,* the Fifth Circuit rejected Pan Am's claim that its practice of hiring only female cabin attendants involved a BFOQ exception.[7] The trial court found that the airline's passengers overwhelmingly preferred to be served by female stewardesses. It also found that the requirement that the attendant be a female was the best available tool for screening out unsatisfactory applicants and thus for improving the average level of performance. In addition, Pan Am introduced psychiatric testimony that the psychological needs of the passengers are better attended to by females. The Fifth Circuit argued that discrimination based on sex is valid only when the essence of the business would be undermined by not hiring one sex. The court then set out the essence of a stewardess position. It asserted that the primary function of an airline is to transport passengers safely from one point to another. It then reasoned that since men are no less able than women to promote this function, being female was not a BFOQ. The Fifth Circuit stated that while women were better able than men to provide the non-mechanical functions of the job relating to a pleasant environment and a desired cosmetic effect, these functions do not relate to the essence of the position.[8]

In *PGA Tour, Inc. v. Martin,* a plaintiff suffering from a degenerative circulatory disorder brought suit against a professional sponsor of golf tournaments (the PGA) for its refusal to allow him to use a golf cart during a professional golf tournament. The suit was brought under the Americans with Disabilities Act of 1990 (ADA).[9] At issue in part was whether allowing Martin to use a golf cart would change the essential aspect of the competition. While this is not strictly an employment condition, the qualifications for competition in the tournament might be seen as analogous to job qualifications. The Supreme Court held that the use of the cart would not change the essence of the sport of golf. It cited several reasons in support of its conclusion. First, it argued that walking was not part of classic golf and that this was a golf tournament. Second, it argued that the rule was not justified by the value of fairness, since it is impossible to guarantee that all competitors will play under the same conditions or that an individual's ability will be the sole determinant of the outcome. Third, it argued that the fatigue from walking is not significant, hence, Martin's use of a cart would not grant him a significant unfair advantage. The Supreme Court was thus willing to identify the essence of a competition in a way that differed from the tournament sponsor. This is similar to the way in which the Fifth Circuit defined the essence of a job and the related notion of a job qualification in a way that differed from the employer's account.

The question that arises is whether job qualifications (and job essences) can be defined in a way that is independent of employer preferences. The first step in exploring this issue is to investigate the concept of a job qualification.

PART 1
The Job Qualification

THE CONCEPT OF A JOB QUALIFICATION

The concept of a qualification is that of a property that fits a person to a position. In the context of a job qualification, the substantive issues concern the identification of the relevant property. The correct conception of a job qualification (i.e., a substantive account of it) is important because certain normative implications are thought to result from an applicant's being the most qualified. In particular, an applicant's being the most qualified for a job is thought to provide a reason for her to get it and, on some accounts, a claim on her behalf to it. To test these notions, we first need to determine the best conception of a job qualification.

A point about strategy is helpful here. In this part of the chapter I attempt to present an account of the essential conditions of a job, that is, a *metaphysical* claim. My argument will rely in part on *moral* arguments. This seems problematic in that these issues are usually distinct. For example, we often distinguish the issue of what punishment is, a conceptual issue, from the issue of when punishment ought to be imposed, a moral issue. In some cases, however, the essential conditions of something can be understood only after we identify the appropriate conception of it.[10] For instance, whether justice is essential to law rests on arguments for the proper conception of law. These arguments and related intuitions are in part moral, for example, arguments concerning whether the actions of judges *qua* interpreters of law ought to legislate and whether a legal system can regularly fail to publicize the rules it expects the citizenry to obey. A similar thing can be said for other controversial conceptions (e.g., desert and prejudice). The underlying idea is that the essential conditions of a concept can be fully explored only upon the determination of the best substantive account of it.

Consider the following analogy from the philosophy of war. The concept "combatant" is a vague one that depending on the particular conception may or may not include army chaplains, army medics, ordnance officers, civilian armament workers, and recreating soldiers. The essential condition for "combatant" will depend on the preferred conception of it, and this is a function of substantive moral argument. The same is true of the concept "job qualification."

THE CONCEPTION OF A JOB QUALIFICATION

In general terms, a job qualification is one of the set of properties that results in a person being able to perform the tasks constituting a job. The properties may do this with different degrees of mediacy. For instance, for an NFL wide receiver (i.e., football players who play a position that is valued primarily for the ability to catch passes), running very fast is a job qualification. This is so even though it is a relevant property only insofar as it brings about another mediately valuable property, namely, the ability to run fast on scripted plays. This property in turn leads to the player's ability to contribute to his team's success, a property that constitutes his overall qualification for the position (although this rests on another assumption that will become apparent shortly). The relationship between mediately valuable properties may be causal or conceptual. So the ability to run fast over short distances may either cause or include within it the ability to run fast on scripted plays, depending on how one thinks of the former ability. In this case, the ability is probably causal, since the former ability does not contain a feature of the latter, namely, the understanding of the script. Also, note that this account of a job qualification is very broad in that it includes many trivial properties not often associated with job qualifications (e.g., having a brain).

My usage of "job qualification" is designed to pick out cases where a property is closely but not necessarily related to the set of abilities that is required in order for a person to succeed at a job. This usage is designed to track the ordinary use of the term. Hence, on this account, the connection between mediately valuable qualifications need not be a necessary one. For example, we ordinarily consider speed as a qualification for a wide receiver, even though it is not necessary for success at the position. This is because other property combinations (e.g., craftiness or the ability to run precise routes) might also produce success at this position. If one prefers to use job qualification as a necessary condition, then substitute "property that is causally or conceptually relevant to success at a job" where I have used "job qualification."

In making the conception of a job qualification more specific, there are a number of variables. First, is the ability in question that which is had at the time that the job is to be filled or at some later time? Second, how are the relevant tasks to be determined? In particular, are they job-specific or are they capable of being specified in a more general manner? Third, if the tasks are identified via the preferences of a relevant party, then who is this party?

Factor #1: Ability versus Potentiality

The ability that grounds a person's being qualified or the most qualified is one that need not be present at the time that an applicant is hired. The background idea is that ability is a type of capacity, and that capacity need not be held at the time of the hiring. Instead, in some cases, the most qualified one is the person with the greatest potential to develop these abilities. For example, a large law firm may hire a lawyer who just passed the bar exam and who is unable to perform many of the duties of an associate in that law firm. However, the young lawyer may be the most qualified in that she will have a sharper learning curve than her competitors. Unless we want to say that such an applicant was not the most qualified, we should say that her relative qualification is a function of her potential (i.e., the likelihood of her acquiring the requisite ability in the future).

There also arises the question as to whether there is an epistemic notion that is a part of the conception of the most qualified applicant. In particular, we want to know whether the most qualified applicant is the person who actually has the greatest potential or who has the greatest potential given the available (or perhaps known) evidence. A similar problem can arise with regard to capacities. I suggest that the concept of the most qualified applicant does not have this condition. The absence of the epistemic condition allows us to be fallible with regard to the most qualified, either because we ignore or discount some relevant evidence or because our evidence of potentiality is imperfect. Consider the case where NFL scouts judge wide receivers primarily on the basis of their speed rather than focusing on their performance in college. We do not think that a scout is mistaken if he were to remark ruefully, "we thought Jones was the most qualified given our team's offensive scheme yet we were sadly mistaken. Our mistake came as a result of our overemphasis on speed."

In addition, an applicant's qualification also rests on her willingness to work hard. On some accounts, this is simply another capacity, that is, a second-order capacity to exercise a capacity or potentiality.[11] However, the capacity notion may fail to capture the notion that the willingness indicates that it is likely (under normal conditions) that the agent will exercise her first-order capacities. Also, on a libertarian account of free will, such a grouping is misleading, since the willingness to work hard results from an uncaused decision and willing. In contrast, a similar thing need not be said about the capacities and potentialities that relate to job performance. For clarity I will group the willingness to work hard as a separate type of job qualification, although in so doing I do not mean to take a position on whether it is a capacity.

The willingness to work hard together with the relevant capacity or potentiality constitute an overall propensity to perform the tasks constituting a job to a certain degree. The relative propensity of different applicants can be then used to fill out the notion that one applicant is more qualified than another.

When determining the relevant capacity or potentiality, we first need to identify the relevant tasks. It is to this issue that we now turn.

Factor #2: The Nature of the Relevant Tasks

Job-specific tasks. The notion that the tasks are job-specific has an obvious appeal. For example, a firefighter's qualification relates to his ability (or potential) to perform as part of a team that puts out fires. In addition, certain activities seem to have an internal goal.[12] For example, medical care should be given out on the basis of ill health. Since activities have internal goals, it is argued that it is a necessary truth that the activity should be arranged to best fulfill that goal. Similarly, it is argued that since certain goods (and jobs) have a social meaning, the distribution of them (or the tasks that constitute them) should be in accord with this social meaning.[13] The social meaning of an activity is the type of good that the activity produces in the life of a particular collection of people. This account is similar to the internal-goal account, except that the tasks constituting a job are specific to a particular society rather than universal. Since the goods are to be distributed in accord with internal goals or social meanings, a job qualification is thus filled out in terms of ability or potentiality to perform actions that promote distribution in accord with the relevant goal or social meaning. For example, the qualifications of a physician are a function of her ability (or potential) to provide medical treatment to those with ill health. This is an essentialist account of jobs, since it views certain parts of the job (e.g., providing health care to the sick) as being essential, whereas other parts (e.g., generating profits) are inessential. The notion that the social-meaning account can be essentialist rests on the idea that the social meaning individuates job types rather than determining its constituent tasks in a particular society. However, if one adopts the latter view, then this account is not essentialist but still capable of identifying in a particular society what tasks constitute a job.

A strength of these essentialist accounts is that they provide a unified account of the particular tasks that constitute a job. A physician's job tasks may include such things as diagnosing disease, investigating family medical history, eliminating bacterial infection, and setting broken bones. On an essentialist account, these tasks are unified by a particular task (e.g., the promotion of health).

Robert Nozick notes that one problem with these essentialist accounts, and ones like them, is that there needs to be a defense of the claim that goods ought to be distributed in accord with their internal goal or social meaning.[14] Yet it is not clear why this should be the case. Could not a person set up a practice that provides medical care, call it "schmoctoring," and emphasize the maximization of profits rather than the provision of medical services to those with ill health? The latter might be the means to the former, but it would be the former that would be the fundamental goal. In addition, Nozick argues that the notion of an internal goal produces absurd results. For example, is it wrong for a barber to provide his services to those who pay him rather than to those who need their hair cut?[15]

A second problem is that there are reasons of autonomy that conflict with this essentialist account of goods and of a job. Reasons of autonomy involve a sphere in which a person has no (non-volunteerist) duties owed to others.

That is, she has a Hohfeldian liberty to pursue her own ends. This sphere gives a person the space in which to pursue her desires, projects, and personal relationships, thereby carving out a space by which she is able to shape her life, free from interference by moral claims from others.[16] Yet if the occupation of a job obligates a person to serve others without those others contracting for such services, or without the person promising to provide such services, then the area in which the person can shape her own life is lessened. Hence, assuming rights to autonomy, persons ought to be able to attempt to create jobs that have demands that do not track the internal goals or social meaning often thought to be part of a position. For example, one should be permitted to try to be a schmoctor rather than a doctor.

An objector might still assert that an internal goal or a social meaning determines the tasks that constitute a job but think that there should be a fine-grained individuation of job types. The notion that the social meaning should determine the tasks that constitute a job, but that there should be an almost endless array of different job types for a person to adopt, is nearly indistinguishable from the view that persons can construct the demands that constitute a job. The social-meaning account is misleading, since it fails to draw attention to the control an individual has over the tasks that constitute a job, and for that reason, it should be set aside.

One might wonder whether jobs (and employment contracts) have essential conditions at all, rather than merely having multiple conditions that reflect the deal struck by the contracting parties.[17] However, essential conditions are required in order to identify the nature of a particular job, and such an identification is required in order to assess a person's qualification for it and performance while in it. This is especially true given that employment contracts sometimes have implicit conditions whose importance depends on the nature of the job.

One should view jobs as having constituent tasks that are relative to the purposes for which they are done. The relevance of these tasks results from the idea that a worker does many things, but only some of them are relevant to her job.[18] For example, a rock musician produces music and moves in a way to emphasize that music. She also makes noises as her feet strike the ground. The former features of her actions are relevant to her job, while the latter are mere side effects. As argued above, the purpose (or purposes) for which a job is done does not seem to depend on some internal feature of the job type or on the general communal understanding of it. Rather, the purpose (or purposes) for which it is done seems to be a function of the demands of some party. The idea here is that since there are some tasks that are part of a given job, and since these tasks are mind-dependent, there must be some person (or persons) who determines them. The most likely candidates are the general population, the business's customers, the employee herself, or the employer.

Whose perspective is it that determines the purpose of a job? The general population's view does not determine the essential features of a job, because it is not clear why the view of persons who are not likely to receive the benefits of the employee's or her employer's services should influence the nature of a job. The people who stand a reasonable chance of occupying or benefiting from the job should determine its relevant contours, and the general population is too broad a category to fill this role.

Perhaps, however, it is the customers whose conception of or preference with regard to a job determines its essential conditions. The notion that it is the view of the customers that determines the tasks that form the essence of a job has a certain plausibility. We think that persons go to a doctor to receive medical treatment, and as a result, the job of the doctor is to provide medical services. We have an analogous view of attorneys, accountants, teachers, etc. This is not a case of a suppressed internal-goal or social-meaning account, since these need not be a function of the customers' view.

One problem with this is the order of explanation. One might think that it is because a doctor's essential task is to provide medical treatment or an attorney's essential task is to provide legal advice and representation that persons go to doctors or attorneys. If this is the case, then it is the nature of the job that determines why customers go to people who occupy them rather than vice versa.

A second problem is that not all persons go into a field to serve the preferences or desires of others. For example, an author might enjoy the process of creating fine literature, with the satisfaction of her fan base being, at most, a distant concern. Or, a gas station owner may seek profits with the satisfaction of his customers being a means to that end. The view of a job as shaped by the view of the customers denies primacy to the person who creates the position, thereby denying him control over his relation with others to whom he does not stand in a special relationship. Such a result conflicts with the existence of above-mentioned reasons of autonomy, in that it does not allow a person options with regard to her relation to others.

This concern for reasons of autonomy does not, however, lead to the employee's views determining the nature of a job. This is because the job involves the employer's property, hence, allowing an employee to shape the employer's relation to others through the use of the employer's property fails to respect his intrinsic value. The underlying idea here is that there is a close relation between a person's property rights and her claims against maltreatment at the hands of other moral agents.

The remaining plausible candidate whose views determine the tasks that constitute a job is the employer. On this account, the person who owns the business determines the tasks that are essential to a job, thereby determining the qualifications of a job. There are several advantages to this account. First, it handles the difference in jobs that seems to accompany the various purposes of employers. It explains why a partnership designed to maximize profit will have different tasks for junior attorneys than one designed to maximize quality representation available to the inner-city poor (e.g., only the former will be asked to assess the resources of a prospective client). Second, it fits with an emphasis on autonomy. As part of their autonomy, persons can create jobs that focus on different things. In particular, jobs may differ on whether they aim at producing pleasure, promoting the good, or other things that are in our interest, regardless of whether they bring pleasure or are desired (e.g., knowledge). They also differ to the extent to which they involve sensitivity to the emotional life of others, emotional identification among a business's members, etc. On this view of jobs, they are relationships with others that in turn have the intrinsic character assigned to them by the persons who own the property that creates them. Jobs, then, are in effect tools by which an employer can structure his world and pursue various projects. This notion of a job as a tool also applies to self-employment, since the relationships involve not just the employer-employee relationship but also the employee-customer relationship.

On this account, since the tasks that constitute a job relate to the employer's preferences, the relevant tasks are those that satisfy the employer's job-specific preferences. The most qualified applicant, on this account, is the one who maximally satisfies these preferences. This last condition screens out cases where one employee is less effective at work than a second employee but adds more to the satisfaction of the employer's preferences via vigorous lovemaking. However, the condition is quite weak, since it screens out only those goals and the means to those goals that the employer views as not part of her business. The condition is therefore subjective, although this is unsurprising given my view of a job as a tool by which an employer pursues certain projects. This maximization condition allows for prioritization where there are conflicting preferences. Thus the most qualified applicant is the one with a capacity or potentiality to perform in a way that maximally satisfies an employer's preferences and a willingness to exercise the capacity or develop the potentiality.[19]

An objector might deny that deontological reasons determine employment conditions. He might assert that the system in which free-market negotiations determine employment conditions is solely justified by the desirable results it brings about. The problem with this objection is that we intuitively distinguish the issue of a person's qualification for a position from the issue of whether better consequences are achieved by giving it to him (and the issue of whether the state should interfere with private employment decisions). For example, imagine that Pan Am is deciding whether to hire Fred or Pam for its last spot on its New York to Tokyo route, and that Pam is more popular among the passengers as well as being safer and more efficient than Fred. However, Fred is a single father without many job options, and better consequences result if he gets the job. It intuitively seems that Pam is more qualified, even if we think that Fred ought to get the job because he needs it to support his family, and that the state should not interfere with Pan Am's hiring decisions. These intuitions are strong ones and should be rejected only reluctantly, especially since neither the consequentialist project nor conceptual clarity requires it.

Two Objections to the Employer-Centered Conception

Objection #1: My Account Ignores the Autonomy of the Employee

An objector might claim that I have ignored the autonomy of the employee. He might assert that the employee's autonomy ought to be given at least as much respect as that of the employer. He might continue that if I account for the exclusive concern for the employer's autonomy in terms of the assumption that employers have unrestricted private property rights, then my argument is trivial, because it would then amount to the claim that the employers determine the essential properties of jobs because they alone own the means of production.

My account need not assume that persons have unrestricted property rights, since the argument works even if there are restrictions (e.g., a ban on inheritance). Nor does the theory depend on private property rights, since on a collectivist account of rights, job qualifications would be a function of the collective, job-specific preferences. A related concern is how the reasons of autonomy come into play in the context of an artificial entity such as a corporation. The reasons of autonomy for a cooperative enterprise are not mysterious; they relate to the aggregate moral space of the shareholders. The unified corporate project that is protected by the shareholders' autonomy requires that persons be capable of having a shared intent and coordinating their actions in support of the intended goal, and neither seems especially problematic.

Objection #2: The Focus on the Employer's Preferences Is a Trivial Result of a Capitalist Account of Private Property

Still, the objector might assert that the focus on the employer's preferences alone trivially results from the distribution of private property rights. This objection seems to get the order of explanation wrong. It is autonomy that justifies an employer's private property rights rather than vice versa.[20] In the sense that warrants protection, autonomy is a state in which a person has adopted, prioritized, and identified with her beliefs and desires, where these beliefs and desires are coherent and the beliefs are substantially true. Since the autonomy is intimately related to the control and use of external objects, the value of the autonomy justifies private property rights. Focusing on the autonomy of the employee in this context would deprive persons of options to shape their interpersonal relationships through the use of objects. While a focus on employees might increase the autonomy of some, it would as an empirical matter lessen overall autonomy by undermining an invaluable class of options.

Another objection to my theory is that a job qualification must take into account the moral appropriateness of the employer's (or other parties') preferences.[21] On this view, for example, a female gynecologist is more qualified than her male counterpart who has equivalent medical skills if the employer's (or perhaps the clientele's) preference for the former is morally appropriate. In contrast, the employer's (or perhaps the bar patrons') preference for a white bartender does not result in whiteness being a job qualification, because the preference is morally inappropriate. On this account, the attributes that make a candidate the most qualified depend on the morality of the employer's (or other parties') preferences. The problem with this account is that it commits us to viewing job qualifications as morally appropriate or perhaps morally appropriate given a particular job, when this does not account for many of our intuitions. For example, we speak of the job qualifications for a hit man, a leader of the Ku Klux Klan, and an investigator for a racy tabloid. If this account were to be correct, then such speech would be confused, and it does not seem to be.

Some persons report not having the intuition that there is a job qualification for these positions.[22] However, it is not clear what this denial rests on, since these positions intuitively seem to be jobs regardless of whether we think of them as morally appropriate. For example, we might disapprove of an investigative reporter whose role is to photograph the private moments of celebrities, dig through their trash, etc. but still recognize that he holds a job. And persons differ in their propensity to perform these tasks.

Given this account of a job qualification, we are now in a position to determine whether there is a moral reason to hire the best-qualified applicant.

PART 2
The Best Conception of a Job Qualification Yields at Most a Very Weak Reason to Favor a Meritocracy

A number of authors argue for meritocracy (i.e., a system where jobs are assigned to the most qualified persons or applicants) in the economic context and in discussing affirmative action.[23] Here I am equating a duty to hire on meritocratic grounds with the duty to hire the most qualified applicant. The concern for merit is at the heart of some of the historical arguments for antidiscrimination laws, such as those banning discrimination on the basis of race, national origin, sex, disability, or age.[24] It also plays a crucial role in some of the arguments for capitalism. In this section I argue that if the duty to hire the most qualified exists at all, then it is quite weak.

It is worth beginning by noting that information-gathering costs limit what employers can learn of prospective employees. As a result, the most qualified person for a job is not always hired. Still this deviation from the alleged duty does not entail that the duty does not exist, or that it would not be better to satisfy it to a greater degree.

Given that the employer is trying to hire someone who is likely to maximally satisfy his preferences, he has a strong incentive to hire the most qualified. This is particularly true given that his preferences may focus on either his own welfare or the welfare of others. An example of the latter occurs where an employer at the Red Cross has preferences that focus on the promotion of the welfare of the poor. However, there are possible cases where out of error, emotion, or for ideological or altruistic reasons an employer hires an applicant who is not the most qualified. For example, a parking garage owner might recognize that a reliable and courteous black employee will likely maximally satisfy his preferences but still have such visceral dislike for black persons that he refuses to hire him. Another example might occur where a partner in a law firm refuses to hire a young lawyer who grew up in an ultra-wealthy family out of a sense of loyalty to his working-class roots. He does so even though he recognizes that his refusal will set back his own interests and do nothing for the working class with whom he identifies. Such cases are similar to weakness-of-the-will cases where a person fails to act upon the outcome of his reasoned deliberation. In the absence of a duty to hire the most qualified candidate, it might still be the case that meritocracy is valuable; however, this need not enter into the deliberation of an employer or a legislator. The plausible arguments for meritocracy focus on rights, desert, fairness, or welfare promotion.

The Right-Based Argument

At least in a private context, the most qualified applicant would not seem to have a right to be hired. A central element in such a right would be a duty owed by the employer to the most qualified applicant. It is hard to see how an applicant could be owed a job based on her having the greatest overall propensity to satisfy the employer's preferences. Nothing about this property suggests that it might ground a duty in another.

This duty may be reflexive, that is, held by and owed to the employer. The idea here is that the employer owes it to himself to hire the most qualified worker, perhaps as a result of a duty to promote his own flourishing.

However, reflexive duties are generally weak or waivable. Thus, for example, one does not consider it a significant wrong to fail to pursue excellence in the employment context, especially where this failure results from the pursuit of hedonic or altruistic goals. The weakness of reflexive duties results from their infringement being a lesser affront to a person's autonomy and dignity than the infringement of interpersonal duties.[25] Hence, even if there is a reflexive duty on the employer to hire the most qualified applicant, the duty is a weak one.

There may be a duty to prospective applicants based on the legitimate expectations that they have formed on the basis of representations by the employer. These expectations generate a duty based on the notion that the representation included a promise to hire the most qualified applicant. Job advertisements or other representations generate a duty only if they make a statement promising to hire the applicant with the greatest propensity to satisfy the employer's preferences. A meritocrat might claim that in the absence of an explicit statement to the contrary, this is an implicit condition. As an empirical matter, I suspect that this is usually not the case, but if I am wrong, then such a duty will rest on the promise implicit in the employer's offer.[26] In any case, the duty will be a promissory one, and thus one that is capable of being eliminated in future cases by an explicit statement to the contrary.

A concern with my account is that it seems to apply only to the type of business where a single person owns the firm and does the hiring. In the corporate world, there seems to be an argument for hiring the most qualified: many people who do the hiring in modern capitalist market economies are acting as agents for others to whom they have contractual duties. Those duties include the duty to hire the person who has the greatest propensity to promote the shareholders' interests. This seems correct but not in conflict with the above arguments, since nothing in this chapter suggests that there are not widespread contractual (or promissory) obligations to hire the most qualified applicant.

The Desert-Based Argument

The hiring of the most qualified might be justified by the applicant's desert. The idea would be that the most qualified applicant usually is the one who worked the hardest to develop her skills. The background notion is that it is intrinsically valuable to give a person what she deserves and that there is often, if not always, a reason to bring about intrinsically valuable states of affairs. On this account, the connection between being the most qualified and the most deserving is contingent and admits of exceptions due to genetic and environmental factors that result in the most qualified not always being the person who has worked the hardest to develop her or his qualifications. The underlying ideas here are that in the economic realm, moral desert tracks hard work, sacrifice, contribution, or some combination of these, and that in the context of a person who has yet to work for an employer, the hard work element is the likely ground for desert.

An objection to this account is that there is no argument as to why in the economic realm a person's deserving something grounds a duty in another.[27] Unless there is a general duty to bring about intrinsically valuable states of affairs, the fact that a person deserves something will not by itself give rise to a duty in others to bring about that state. Such a general duty conflicts with the existence of a sphere of discretion created by reasons of autonomy. Where, for instance, two quarterbacks of approximately equal ability compete for a starting position on an NFL team, but one has far greater desert than the other, it intuitively seems that the owner does not wrong the more deserving candidate if he decides not to consider his relative desert. However, if justice in the employment context does track moral desert, and if the most qualified candidate is on average the most deserving, then the case for meritocracy becomes stronger.

George Sher puts forth an argument in favor of the notion that the most qualified has a desert-based claim to a position. This duty in others rests on the general duty to treat all persons as rational agents and the notion that the ability reflects the exercise of an agent's agency, especially her practical reasoning.[28] Sher's assumptions are that practical reason encompasses the decision and resulting acts to develop one's skills, and that respecting a person's practical reasoning abilities involves respecting the exercise of practical reason. This duty conflicts with the moral space that is grounded by a person's autonomy, since the duty would not allow him to structure his workplace relationship with others as he sees fit. Since Sher's hypothesized duty seems to be grounded by autonomy, I suspect that it does not exist.

The Fairness Argument

A claim of fairness, like the concern about universality, is a formal notion in that it is parasitic upon either other values such as rights and desert or other factors such as contribution and sacrifice. For example, a claim that a mechanic in a body shop is unfairly paid is usually filled out in terms of his deserving more pay given his hard work or his meriting more pay given his contribution to the business. I have already argued that rights and desert cannot support meritocracy. Nor is there a close enough linkage between being the most qualified applicant and either contribution or sacrifice to ground a fairness-based claim. Hence, fairness does not provide a reason to hire on merit-based grounds.

The Welfare Argument

On some accounts, consequentialist arguments provide support for a duty to hire the most qualified person. These consequentialist arguments may, depending on the account one adopts, involve such factors as desert satisfaction, right fulfillment, or the collective welfare of persons. Meritocracy is sometimes thought to maximize this last type of value.[29] In a macro-job assignment, the overall assignment of persons to jobs is done in a way that best achieves a system-wide goal (e.g., welfare maximization). For example, a system in which racial minorities are assigned jobs over more qualified applicants may be justified on utilitarian grounds.

If one accepts consequentialism, then there is a strong reason to accept a duty to engage in macro-job assignments. Even on a nonconsequentialist account, some value may be placed on efficiency or beneficence, at least to the extent that they are not undermined or overridden by reasons of autonomy, hence, a case in support of a macro-job assignment can be made. However, even if these arguments are sound, they do not support a meritocracy, since this need not track a macro-job assignment. The strength of the consequentialist argument increases considerably, however, with regard to jobs that are directly connected to the safety of other persons (e.g., airline pilots, heart surgeons, and bridge designers).[30]

Since these are the most plausible accounts of the duty to hire the most qualified applicant, and since these accounts do not succeed, there is probably no such duty. If this is correct, then significant implications follow with regard to antidiscrimination laws.

PART 3
Antidiscrimination Laws Cannot Be Justified by Meritocratic Concerns

Antidiscrimination laws are often justified on the basis of fairness. Fairness is then filled out via the notion that hiring ought to be based on traditional views of merit. The discrimination need not reflect the employer's attitudes. For example, a law firm might refuse to hire a black or a Puerto Rican applicant not because of the prejudice on behalf of the law firm's partners but rather because the firm's clients refuse to have their work handled by members of these groups.[31]

Such laws are often thought to promote fair hiring practices in a way that does not put any particular business at a competitive disadvantage. Other rationales are also put forth in support of such laws, although I leave them aside, since they are outside the scope of this chapter.

To the extent that antidiscrimination laws prevent businesses from hiring persons who maximize the satisfaction of the employer's job-related preferences, such laws block merit-based hiring. For example, consider the case where a security firm (e.g., it provides night watchmen) is composed of partners whose foremost concern in forming the partnership was and is to maximize profits. Antidiscrimination laws force the firm to hire a black man who, because of racist clients, prevents profit maximization. The firm is thus forced to hire persons other than the most qualified applicants.

This fact holds true regardless of whether these laws are universally enforced, because given the racist preferences of the clientele, the firm is at a competitive disadvantage relative to firms for whom the most qualified applicant happens by chance not to be a black person.

Race can also be a qualification for a job. Consider an example where a counseling business is hired by the U.S. government to set up centers for domestic abuse victims on reservations and where Native American women find it much easier to talk to a Native American therapist about such matters. Being Native American is a qualification, because it is a property that enables a person to satisfy more effectively the employer's goals (i.e., providing psychological counseling to a specific group of vulnerable women). That it does so by producing another property (i.e., being easier for Native American women to talk to) does not prevent it from being a qualification.

The nature of a job qualification requires different reasoning in the civil rights cases. It requires that the laws be interpreted as overriding the employer's choice for the person who is probably the most qualified applicant. It also requires in the context of BFOQs that the courts avoid reasoning about the essence of a job in a way that is independent of the employer's preferences. For example, the *Diaz* court's attempt to define the essence of a cabin flight attendant should be seen for what it is: a policy- or principle-based plan to force the airline to hire, on average, less-qualified employees. That is not to say that the law and the federal courts' interpretation of it are unjustified, but rather that we should be clear about what is being done.

In this chapter, I have focused on private employers. In the context of state employment, the conception of merit is the same. The range of morally permissible preferences is more restricted than in the private field, although whether the moral restrictions affect the actual qualifications for a job (as opposed to what ought to be the qualifications for it) is a tricky issue that I discuss in the next chapter.

PART 4
Qualifications for Educational Institutions

A student in an educational program in some ways resembles a business customer because she or a third party pays the educational institution to receive goods and services rather than being paid to provide them. And it is not clear that there is a most qualified customer. At the same time, we have a clear sense in which some applicants for an educational position are more qualified than their competitors. For example, a student who applies to a premier engineering school (e.g., Massachusetts Institute of Technology) and who excels at math, physics, and computer science intuitively seems more qualified than a student who is similar except for his having difficulty in those areas.

If an educational institution is viewed as a tool by which an owner tries to promote certain goals, then an applicant's qualification can be filled out in terms of her propensity to satisfy these goals. An applicant's propensity is a function of her willingness to work hard together with the relevant capacity or potentiality.[32] On this account, the notion of a qualification for an educational institution is similar to that for a job. If an applicant's qualification is a function of the owner's goals, then the propensity to learn, play football, or help minority communities is a qualification to the extent that it promotes the owner's goal or goals. Where the owner is a collection of persons (e.g., a state's citizenry), the goal is restricted to the common goal had for it by the collection (or at least a substantial portion of it). Thus where citizens of a state support a university as a means by which to promote knowledge in areas important to self-understanding and citizenship, this goal is the one by which to judge an applicant's qualifications. Other valuable traits on this account (e.g., the ability to play football or contribute to racial diversity) are not qualifications.

The argument here, like the argument with regard to job qualifications, is that this account of a qualification coheres with the concept of a job qualification, an emphasis on the autonomy of the owners, and our intuitions with regard to particular cases. This picture has great intuitive appeal. It explains why the most qualified applicant for a premier science school (e.g., California Institute of Technology) might not be the most qualified applicant for a premier military academy (e.g., West Point) or a religious college (e.g., Bob Jones University).

State and private educational institutions probably do not have as their fundamental goals such things as football victories, the promotion of alumni families, the creation of wealthy individuals, or the promotion of diversity or equal opportunity. This can be seen by considering what the owners consider these institutions' fundamental goal and the conditions under which they would withdraw consent to them (i.e., the goals that if frustrated would lead to the withdrawal of consent). Evidence in favor of my empirical claim includes the stated fundamental goals of state colleges and universities and the widespread view that they are designed to promote certain types of knowledge. Other goals may still be viewed as the means by which the more fundamental goals are achieved. However, unless they are part of the owners' (i.e., citizens') consciously adopted means by which to achieve the fundamental goals, it is an empirical question whether they actually are the most effective means (or part of the most effective means) by which the larger goal is achieved. Here I will assert but not defend the notion that the lowered learning potentiality that characterizes beneficiaries of strong affirmative action hinders rather than promotes the conveyance of the relevant types of knowledge to students. This is in part because the beneficiaries of strong affirmative action are, on average, less able to grasp important concepts and arguments, more likely to drop out, and more likely to slow down the rate of learning in other students than do non-beneficiaries.[33] I have no clear sense as to whether the same can be said of close relations between alumni and a university or of a high-visibility football program.

An objector might assert that educational institutions, unlike employment ones, include diversity and equal opportunity among their fundamental goals. He might note that the colleges and universities mention them as goals. This objection fails if the goals of diversity and equal opportunity are mere enhancements to the university's fundamental mission. The fundamental goals of colleges and universities are to produce knowledge, the ability to think about different issues, or the results of such states, for example, increased well-being. The same colleges and universities existed before diversity and equal-opportunity goals were added, which suggests that the latter are not part of the institution's defining purpose or purposes. The institutions' owners probably understand these more recent goals as having a loose connection to the institutions' defining purpose or purposes. This last point rests on the psychological claim that the institutions' owners would probably think that under changed conditions the institutions are worth preserving, even where they become unable to promote diversity or equal opportunity.[34] This is analogous to the way in which the citizenry would probably think that the police are worth preserving, even where this cannot be done in a way that promotes diversity and equal opportunity. If this is correct, then diversity is not a fundamental or even a mid-level goal for colleges and universities but at most a consideration that guides the pursuit of these goals. And it is not true even if such concerns were adopted in an attempt to ward off lawsuits based on federal law rather than on the basis of the citizenry's preference.

Thus the most qualified applicant for an educational institution is that student with the propensity to maximally satisfy the institution owners' preferences. A student's contribution to diversity is in general not one of these capacities or potentialities. Hence, it seems that even with my inclusive criterion for qualifications, a student's contribution to campus diversity is probably not an educational qualification.

PART 5
Conclusion

The most qualified applicant is the one who has the propensity to maximally satisfy the employer's preferences. An applicant's propensity is a function of her willingness to work hard together with the relevant capacity or potentiality to do the tasks constituting a job. Given this account of the most qualified applicant, there is only a weak duty, if any, to hire persons on the basis of their being the most qualified. Such a duty is not justified by reference to rights, desert, fairness, or the maximization of welfare. However, such a duty may come about via promises made by the employer or the employee who does the hiring. These results suggest that antidiscrimination laws cannot be justified on the basis of merit, although other justifications might still be available.

SECTION 3

Strong Affirmative Action

2

Strong Affirmative-Action Programs at State Institutions

PART 1
Introduction

THESIS

An act of strong affirmative action involves giving preference to minority and women candidates who are less qualified than others, usually with regard to a job, an educational opportunity, or some other benefit.[1] Strong affirmative action is currently practiced in the academic world by many state educational institutions. Given the finding in the last chapter that there probably is no duty to hire the most qualified applicant, and thus no right of the most qualified to be hired, one might think that this is clearly permissible. However, this case gets more complex because of the presence of a state agent distributing state resources such as a job or subsidized education. I have chosen to focus on state educational institutions because I think they best illustrate the principles involved in a state's strong affirmative-action programs. The same principles apply to hiring state workers and giving out other state-financed benefits. The only difference is that the forward-looking benefits that I leave out of this discussion (e.g., diversity) seem much less attractive in these other areas.

Among the most widely cited moral justifications for strong affirmative action are the values of compensatory (or corrective) justice and the value of diversity. Diversity and compensatory justice are not the only moral reasons that might be claimed to support strong affirmative action. Strong affirmative action might also be justified by desert, consequentialism, virtue (either of the community or of the administrators of the educational programs), etc. or some combination of these reasons. The compensatory justice justification is captured in (1).

(1) Other things being equal, a state educational institution may choose to hire a less qualified candidate over a more qualified candidate, because the weight given to the race or gender of the less qualified candidate relates to the elimination of a debt of compensatory justice.

The "other things being equal" phrase indicates that the elimination of a debt of compensatory justice functions as a moral reason, although not necessarily a sufficient moral reason for strong affirmative action.

I will argue that (1) is probably false. First, I shall specify the conflict between the interests and desert of a white male and the compensatory justice claim of a woman or a racial minority. Second, I shall look at three different attempts to make out the claim that compensatory justice provides an argument for choosing lesser-qualified persons. I shall argue that none of these attempts work. Since the three most plausible attempts to provide a compensatory justice justification for strong affirmative-action programs at state educational institutions fail, I conclude that (1) is probably false. My argument does not entail that (1) is false. But the failure of representative experts in a field to come up with a successful theory supporting a particular type of claim is evidence against that type of claim being true. In this case, the failure of philosophers to come up with a justification for (1) based on more general moral principles is evidence against the truth of (1).

Caveats

Some caveats are in order. First, I shall focus on race and gender. Affirmative action might also be thought to be justified with regard to ethnicity, physical or mental disability, disadvantaged socioeconomic backgrounds, sexual orientation, etc. For the purposes of limiting discussion, I shall focus on these two variables, although the conclusions of this analysis can be generalized to these other cases.

Second, I shall rely on the previous analysis of the notion of the most qualified applicant as the applicant who has the propensity to maximally satisfy the employer's preferences. Nevertheless, a few comments are in order with regard to the notion of qualification. In some cases, race or gender improves performance. For example, if a Native American counselor is better able to work with Native American students because the students identify with her, then her race or ethnic background is a qualification, just as an attribute of a clinical psychologist that enables her to create an empathetic environment is a qualification for a clinical psychologist.[2] Where an applicant's race or gender relates to performance, that applicant's race or gender is a qualification, hence, consideration of the applicant's race or gender is not to be considered part of a strong affirmative-action program. However, where race and gender do not relate to performance, one applicant is more qualified than another applicant if and only if the former, on the basis of her attributes, should be chosen over the latter were the two to be members of all of the same demographic groups. The attributes that turn out to be qualifications depend on the goals that the state ought to pursue. For example, whether racial and ethnic preference is an educational qualification will depend on the relative importance of the state promoting students' social ease with other racial and ethnic groups in comparison to knowledge about the great historical events and philosophical works of Western civilization. I argued in chapter 1 that educational institutions ought to promote knowledge that allows persons to shape their lives and function as effective citizens.

Third, I shall focus on the state as the agent of strong affirmative-action programs. Concerns about the freedom of association, private property, and the freedom of expression may prevent certain discriminatory act-types from infringing on rights in the private sector but still result in their being impermissible when performed by a governmental entity. For example, these concerns may make it permissible for a group of Korean Americans to band together and give out a scholarship reserved exclusively for Korean Americans, while such actions would be impermissible for a government entity. In order to screen out these concerns, I shall focus on state actions.

PART 2
The Duty to Judge Persons According to Their Interests and Desert

COMPENSATORY JUSTICE AS A COMPETING INTEREST

In the context of distributing state resources that have been taken via coercion (i.e., via taxes), the following rule (2) applies.

> (2) Other things being equal, if preference for one individual over another individual is justified, then the interests of the first with regard to the state resources are more important.

The "other things being equal" phrase screens out concerns for the third-party interests that might provide a sufficient moral reason to favor one of the competing individuals.

The idea here is where people are coerced and not allowed to use their own judgment on how to transfer resources and opportunities, there is a corresponding moral duty that the coercion be implemented in a way that respects persons' rights and takes their interests and desert into account. Underlying this idea is the notion that the state is justified through either actual consent of the citizens or the duty of fair play.[3] It is doubtful that persons would consent to the state were it to reserve the right to use coercion in ways that do not respect persons' other rights or that are not justifiable in terms of persons' interests and desert. The duty of fair play in this context involves a justification of state authority that involves the generation of a duty in members of a mutually beneficial and just enterprise that fairly distributes the burdens and benefits of the enterprise. This account presupposes that the relevant burdens, such as being subject to coercion, be fairly distributed. Fairness is a formal value that is properly cashed out in terms of the impartial consideration of persons' interests (and on some accounts desert and rights). Hence, it is the justification of the state that supports (2).

There are different ways an interest can be understood. The three most plausible theories regarding an interest are hedonistic theories, which assert that what is in someone's interest is what would make a person's life the happiest, where happiness is understood as the psychological state of pleasure; desire-fulfillment theories, which assert that what is in a person's interest is what would best fulfill a person's desires; or objective list theories, which assert that what is in one's interest are a number of things that are conceptually distinct from one's pleasure or desires.[4] Objective list theories may view a person's interests as including that person receiving what she is owed as a matter of justice.

In effect, (2) is asserting that a person ought, other things being equal, to be treated as an individual with regard to the receipt of coercively taken resources. A person is treated as an individual if and only if her treatment directly (conceptually) relates to either her interest or what she deserves.[5] The idea here is that if a treatment does not directly relate to a person's interest or desert, then it is not closely enough related to anything that is identifiably hers, and hence does not focus on her as an individual.

Treatment based on some attributes (e.g., membership in certain race and gender classes) does not, by itself, conceptually relate to a significant interest or desert. For example, simply because Jane is a woman or a black does not, by itself, mean that she has a legitimate claim of compensatory justice or has performed an act (or omission) that deserves reward. Hence, if the treatment of a person is based on an attribute such as race or gender, then she is not treated as an individual. And to the extent that her treatment is based in part on such an attribute, then to that extent she is not treated as an individual.

The interests of one individual are more important than the interests of another individual only if there is a morally relevant difference between the two individuals. Hence, other things being equal, if preference for one individual over another individual is justified with regard to state educational resources, then there is a morally relevant difference between the two individuals.

If there is a morally relevant difference between two individuals competing for scarce resources at state educational institutions, then this difference is not likely to be the result of being the member of a racial or gender group. This is because being a member of different race or gender groups does not, by itself, constitute or entail a morally relevant difference between individuals. Membership in a racial or gender group may be evidence of a moral difference, such as being the victim of unjust racial discrimination or suffering the effects of such acts on others. But here the morally relevant difference is a significant interest that is connected to racial or gender group membership only via the concern for administrative efficiency. To the extent that gender or race is closely related to the harm a person suffers through unjust discrimination against her or her ancestor, the relevant interest becomes unjustly-injured-and-hence-owed compensation[6]

This can be seen, for instance, in that someone else who suffers the same type of harm but who suffered discrimination against her or her ancestor because of her religious views ought to receive the same compensation as the person who suffered because of her or her ancestor's gender or race. To the extent that both types of cases involve the same type of unjust discriminatory acts and the same type of injury, it is the acts and the injury, not the race, gender, or religion, that justifies compensatory treatment. Hence, race and gender remain morally irrelevant, even though they may be helpful indicators of which persons ought to receive compensation.

Thus strong affirmative-action programs in state educational institutions will turn out to be morally justified by compensatory justice only if the interest of compensatory justice constitutes a strong enough moral value to override the white male's interest or desert as related to the educational opportunity.

THE DUTY ACCOMPANYING INTERESTS AND DESERT

There is a duty accompanying a person' s desert and educational interest with regard to educational positions. In the context of a position at a state educational institution, on average, the white male has a greater desert and possibly a greater educational interest.

The white male is, by hypothesis, more qualified for the educational position. If we assume that, on average, more qualified persons for a position have worked harder, then it follows that the white male will have worked harder, hence, he is more deserving of the position than his female or black competitor. This assumption tracks our ordinary assumptions. For example, we ordinarily assume that, on average, students with higher grade point averages worked harder than those with lower ones. Similarly, we assume that, on average, the persons who win a marathon race have worked harder than those entrants who do not win the race. These claims are empirical ones, and a more in-depth defense of them is beyond the scope of this chapter.

This assumption is obviously quite controversial. It rests on the further assumption that there is not a significant genetic difference between white males as opposed to women and blacks or, more specifically, a large enough difference to negate the general presumption that the more qualified person, on average, has worked harder. It also rests on the assumption that the environment that women and blacks face is not so hostile as to make approximately equal amounts of effort produce vastly different developments in skill or knowledge. Note that if a hostile environment lowers the qualifications of women and blacks by lowering their willingness to work and if, as I claim, desert tracks actual work, then my claim is not refuted.

If we identify actual work as the weighted product of the type and number of praiseworthy acts, then desert should attach to one's actual work. Generally, outside of punishment, desert is thought to track contribution, ability, or actual work (i. e., effort). In fact, desert should be seen to track only actual work for two related reasons. First, work is least affected by factors outside of the agent's control. For example, one's contribution may depend on the surrounding work environment, an environment over which one may have little control. Similarly, ability depends in large part on one's genetic makeup and childhood environment, factors over which one has almost no control. In addition, relative ability is dependent in large part on the actual work, genetic makeup, and the surrounding competitive environment, factors over which one has little control.

Second, an agent must be responsible for the ground of a desert claim. To the extent that someone is responsible for anything, that person controls that thing through her acts. Here I will assume that omissions are a type of act. Suppose a woman develops her mathematical abilities and determines her contribution to the field of mathematics through her past acts. Desert ought to rest on what persons are most clearly responsible for. Since persons are most clearly responsible for that which they have the greatest control over, and since they have the greatest control over acts, judgments of desert probably ought to track a person's acts. In contrast, contribution and ability should be seen as evidence of the ground of desert rather than as the actual ground of desert.

At the very least, desert rests in part on an agent's actual work. Since the other suggested grounds of desert can be explained in terms of an agent's actual work, and since work more clearly contains the attribute that is essential to the ground of desert, there is some reason to believe that actual work is the sole ground of desert. Someone might object that this argument for the white male applicant's greater desert is only a statistical generalization that does not always hold true. However, in this respect, claims of desert and interest are on the same footing as the use of race or gender as an indicator of the property of being owed compensation for past injustices, which grounds the compensatory justice claims of women and members of minority groups. Not every woman or black is going to have this property, hence the use of race or gender as an evidential indicator is justified by statistical concerns giving rise to an argument from administrative efficiency. Given a statistical use of evidential indicators, it is not clear that we cannot use similar evidential indicators of a person's degree of desert in an educational position.

One might object that pervasive racism creates such obstacles to skill development that we cannot assume that, on average, black competitors have worked less hard than the best-qualified white males.[7] However, if a racist environment lowers the qualifications of women and blacks by lowering their willingness to work or their actual work, and desert tracks actual work, then my claim that in this context women and blacks will be less deserving of a benefit is not refuted. Even if this is not the only effect of discrimination, it might be prevalent enough to preserve the plausibility of the assumption that the most qualified person has also worked the hardest in pursuit of a benefit. Also, one of the primary effects of past discrimination may be a lessening of control over desires, as evidenced by the high rate of violent crime among black males and the prevalence of out-of-wedlock births in the black community. This would make it seem plausible that past discrimination will have affected the willingness of blacks to work and the actual work they do, since both considerations require significant control over competing desires.

A second objection is that desert attaches to things that are not under a person's control, or at least less under a person's control than actual work. For example, one objector claims that it not only makes sense but also is true to say things such as "I buy a lottery ticket and win, hence, I deserve the prize," despite the fact that a lottery is largely out of one's control. There are several responses to this objection. First, intuitions differ with regard to the case. My intuitions are that the lottery case does not even make sense. However, this response is weakened insofar as it does not reflect a clear interpersonal pattern of intuitions. Second, we may simply call the moral claim type that is grounded by an act, where the act is subject to moral evaluation and is such that an agent is morally responsible for it, control-based desert. The argument can be reformulated in terms of control-based desert without weakening it.

It may be objected that the desert claim is not part of the compensation but a claim competing against the justice of compensating for unjustly caused losses, and that the burden is not disproportionate. The problem with this objection is that overriding the best-qualified person's legitimate desert claim is the best candidate for the burden of compensation. If overriding the desert claim is not the burden of compensation and the best-qualified person does not suffer a violation of rights, and no other person shoulders the burden of compensation, then we are left with the conclusion that strong affirmative-action programs do not place the burden of compensation on anyone. This is implausible, since something of value seems to be transferred to the minority or woman candidate.

Also, one might think that a more qualified student is likely to have a greater educational interest in a state educational program. This is because he is more likely to succeed in it, thereby increasing the chances of his investment of time and resources being rewarded, of his important desires being satisfied, and of his experiencing the pleasures resulting from his completion of the program. Also, because he is more qualified, he is more likely to learn more in the classroom. And to the extent that knowledge is intrinsically valuable, and more knowledge has more intrinsic value, his increased knowledge will be more intrinsically valuable.

There is also a duty accompanying women's and minorities' interests in the rectification of unjust injury or the effects of unjust injury. The duty corresponding to desert and educational interests and the duty corresponding to a compensatory-justice interest may conflict, insofar as they may be owed to different persons. Note that the conflict is not a conflict as to whether or not one of the competitors is to be treated as an individual, since both persons are considered on the basis of his or her significant interests or desert. Also note that consideration of the duty to give persons equal consideration is not helpful in this context, since we have three types of grounds for duties: desert, educational interests, and compensatory-justice interests, and only after we have determined their relative importance can we determine what constitutes equal consideration.

Strong affirmative-action programs at state educational institutions in effect reject the duty to always give the educational position to the person who, on average, has a greater desert and possibly a greater educational interest. Thus we must determine if there is a type of situation where the compensatory-justice interest overrides either of these or similar interests.

PART 3
Strong Affirmative-Action Programs at State Educational Institutions Cannot Be Justified via Compensatory Justice

What Is Compensatory Justice?

Compensatory justice aims at eliminating or rectifying unjustifiable gains and losses. The usual concern of compensation is the nullification of the victim's losses, the reordering of her affairs to make her whole again.[8] It generally relies on a comparison of the actual world in which the injured party lives to a relevantly similar possible world in which this party lives but where the unjust injuring act never occurred.[9] Just compensation places the person in qualitatively the same position she would have been had she lived in the possible world. Since the purpose of the compensatory-justice justification is to place the injured person in the qualitatively same position she would have been in but for the unjust injurious act, the justification requires that we be able to determine the amount of compensation that is necessary to place her in this position.

This test for harm needs to be tightened up, however, since one need not be worse off in this world than in the possible world in which the unjust act did not occur in order to be owed compensation as a matter of justice.[10] To see this, imagine two delinquent boys who agree that the one, A, will push the next innocent bystander into the path of a particular truck, but that if he should fail the other one, B, will then push the bystander into the truck's path. A victim, C, who was pushed into the path of an oncoming truck and was injured as a result of A's push could not legitimately complain that he was better off in the world in which A did not perform his unjust act. This is because he would have been hit by the same truck at the same time even if A did not push him. Compensatory justice, however, still demands that A pay C damages, since C would not have suffered the token harm that he did but for A's act, even though in the absence of A's act, C still ends up with the same type of injuries. The background idea is that the agent who performs an act is an essential property of that act and the harm that that act produces, hence, B could not have performed the same act token as A performed, nor could he have caused the same token harm.[11]

The compensatory justice justification of affirmative action requires the considerations of two central questions. What compensation is owed to the injured party? Who owes the injured party compensation? The compensatory-justice justification of strong affirmative action is a type of backward-looking justification of strong affirmative-action programs. The desert-based justification of such programs are also backward-looking, but are distinguishable from compensatory-justice justifications in that the former but not the latter requires that the relevant act or feature warranting the benefit be under the agent's control.[12]

A series of problems accompanies this counterfactual. First, there are metaphysical problems surrounding the identification and possible nonexistence of the injured person in the possible world.[13] Second, there are serious questions concerning the moral relevance of the injured party's failure to try to alleviate the effects of the unjust injury.[14] This is particularly important where one of the main effects of unjust discrimination is a dampening of persons' willingness to work. Third, in the case of the descendants of American slaves, there are concerns about whether the injuring enslavement brought about benefits to American blacks, specifically the benefits of access to

American education, technology, and wealth that outweigh the costs that resulted from enslavement.[15] For the purposes of this chapter, I shall assume that none of these problems is fatal to the compensatory justice justification.

Two Different Conceptual Questions Surrounding Compensatory Justice Claims

Let us assume that women and minorities are injured through the effects of past discrimination. Two questions accompany any justified claim to compensation on the basis of compensatory justice. First, what amount and type of compensation are owed to the injured party? Second, who owes the injured party compensation? For the purposes of assessing a particular compensation proposal, the second question cannot be answered without reference to the first question.[16] An example from Robert Fullinwider will help illustrate this point.

> Suppose that you have stolen a rare and elaborately engraved hunting rifle from me. Before you can be made to return it, the gun is destroyed in a fire. By coincidence, however, your brother possesses one of the few other such rifles in existence; perhaps it is the only other model in existence apart from the one you stole from me and which was destroyed. From my point of view, having my gun back or having one exactly like it is the best form of compensation I can have from you. No other gun will be a suitable replacement, nor will money serve satisfactorily to compensate me for the loss. I prized the rifle for its rare and unique qualities, not for its monetary value. You can pay me the best form of compensation by giving me your brother's gun. However, this is clearly not a morally justifiable option. I have no moral title to your brother's gun, nor are you (solely in virtue of your debt to me) required or permitted to take your brother's gun to give me. The gun is not yours to give; and nothing about the fact that you owe me justifies you in taking it.[17]

White males have a strong interest in educational opportunity, and in some cases a white male's effort, ability, or contribution gives rise to a strong desert claim to the educational position. The above case (and cases like it) indicates that we can override the duty corresponding to a particular white male's interest or desert claim (thereby requiring him to shoulder the burden of compensation) only if that particular white male owes the injured party compensation.

Other examples, designed to illustrate that these considered moral judgments are part of a general pattern, are easily generated by considering cases where the best form and amount of compensation involve the violation of an innocent person's property rights or a strong moral duty owed to that innocent person. As a result, considered moral judgments generated from the above case can be used to support the more general claim about the close relation between the two questions. Thus we now turn to the question of whether all or most white males owe compensation to racial minorities and women.

WHO OWES THE INJURED PARTY COMPENSATION?

There are three different reasons given as to why the duty owed to white males may justifiably be given lesser weight and the burdens of compensation placed on them. First, white males are morally guilty in that they perpetrated culpable wrongdoings (or omissions) that caused injury, hence, they are not owed the duty corresponding to their interest. Second, white males themselves owe compensation because they are innocent beneficiaries of past unjust discrimination. Third, white males owe compensation because they are members of a community that owes compensation.

Approach #1: White Males Can Be Asked to Pay Compensation because They Are Morally Guilty

The focus on moral guilt has generally not been the focus of the compensatory justice arguments for strong affirmative-action programs. Nevertheless, one reason we might have to give lesser weight to the duties owed to white males is that they have failed to respect similar duties to others. Since, on some accounts, a person is owed a duty only if he is willing to respect that same duty when owed to others, the white male ought not to receive the protection of the duty to respect his interest and desert with regard to state resources.[18] On this account, then, since racial minorities and women are owed compensation, and since the form of compensation, strong affirmative action, does not violate any duty that might be owed to the persons who shoulder the burden of this form of compensation, the compensation ought, other things being equal, to be implemented.

In determining whether or not white males are guilty of failing to recognize or satisfy the duty to respect the interests and desert of non-white males, a useful path is to look at the notion of moral guilt that underlies a finding of legal guilt in the criminal law. In general, a person deserves punishment only if he (1) intentionally, (2) committed a wrongdoing (or omitted to act if omissions are not themselves acts), (3) which ordinarily would cause a harm, and (4) the act (or omission) was performed under circumstances that do not amount to either a justification or an excuse for having caused the harm.[19]

The argument from moral guilt does not support strong affirmative action at state educational institutions because many young white males have not performed the relevant types of culpable wrongdoing (i.e., overt acts of racial or sexual discrimination).

It might be objected that young white males are not so innocent because they have not met their duty to struggle against injustice or the effects of injustice wherever it exists, or because they have engaged in various social and economic practices that tend to perpetuate the inferior socioeconomic position of minorities and women.

One response is that some white males attempted to meet their duty through various political activities. For example, many white males have met this duty by working for candidates who pursue policies that oppose injustice or reverse the inferior position of minorities and women. These policies may consist of free-market solutions, such as the removal of disincentives to work and marriage, a decrease in government interference in persons' lives, or a lessening of government redistribution of income and wealth. What counts as struggling against injustice depends, in part, on one's theory of what policies will tend to eliminate the effects of past and current discrimination.

A person does a culpable wrongdoing only if he has a culpable mental state. To have a culpable mental state, a white male must have performed his wrongdoing (or omission) intentionally.[20] That certain things that are entailed by (or reasonably inferred from) one's intentional acts need not be sufficient for the agent to have a culpable mental state. So for example, checkmating one's opponent may entail the end of a chess game, but if ending the chess game is not what the agent purposely tried to bring about, and if he does not know that the end of the game will come about as a result of his action, then the agent does not intend it.

Hence, a person who in good faith chooses an ineffective policy (or a policy that has counterproductive effects) to combat the effects of past injustices is not a perpetrator of injustice, since he lacks the intent to do harm to minorities and women or to perpetuate the effects of past discrimination. Thus given the complexity of the issues with regard to the effective remediation of past wrongs, a lot of white males who have at least tried in good faith to combat the effects of past unjust acts will not be perpetrators of injustice. If many white males are not culpable wrongdoers, then they have not performed actions that lessen or negate the duty to respect their interest or desert.

Approach #2: White Males Owe Compensation because They Are Innocent Beneficiaries of Past Discrimination

A person might owe compensation for his act even though he does not perform a culpable wrongdoing,[21] for a person can impose unjust costs on others even where that person performs an action that is justified, given the circumstances. So, for example, where a person faced with death by freezing breaks into another's cabin and uses the owner's wood to keep himself alive, the trespasser's acts are justified. Nonetheless, because the trespasser infringed upon the cabin owner's property rights and caused her financial injury, one might think that the trespasser owes the cabin owner compensation.[22]

On approach #2, innocent beneficiaries of past unjust discrimination owe compensation, even if they are morally innocent. This notion is captured by Principle #1.

> Principle #1
>
> Other things being equal, one person, P, ought to pay compensation to injured party, I, if and only if P benefited from an unjust act that injured I.[23]

The problem with Principle #1 is that a person who gains a competitive advantage as the result of others' unjust acts does not necessarily owe compensation. This point can be seen in Case #1.

> Case #1
>
> Jim, a white American, is the second-best tennis player in the world, second only to a Chinese American, Frank. As a result of Frank's superiority, Jim makes only one-third the money that Frank makes. One weekend, however, Frank is out on the town with his white girlfriend and is viciously beaten and stabbed by a racist Brooklyn mob. This mob has no connection to Jim. Jim, now freed of competition from Frank, wins more tennis tournaments, and as a result, his income triples. Jim has thus directly benefited from an injustice done to Frank.
>
> Jim does not perform any culpable act (or omission) that would make him liable for any of Frank's losses. This is particularly true, since Jim does not simply take Frank's lost earnings but must still win them through the disciplined training and hard work that is required in order for a person to win professional tennis tournaments. Hence, Jim is not morally guilty with respect to Frank's injury, since he has committed no wrongdoing (or omission) that is related to the mob's unjust acts.

Principle #1 should be rejected. Another person cannot force obligations on you simply by providing you with benefits, particularly benefits that you would reject if you knew their source. You are liable for compensation only if you actually consented to receive the benefits with adequate knowledge of their origin. However, you need not recognize the origin as being unjust (or unjustified) in order to owe compensation. This is because a mistake as to the moral significance of the appropriating act does not negate one's liability.

Hence, other things being equal, a person is unjustly injured when unearned and unconsented to benefits are taken from him and the taking of these benefits injures him.

To see this let us return to Case #1. You will recall that Jim's earnings tripled as a result of Frank's receiving an unjust beating and stabbing from a Brooklyn mob. My intuitions are that the mob that injured Frank does not thereby produce an obligation on behalf of Jim to compensate Frank, although it might well be a nice gesture on Jim's behalf to donate some money to Frank. More specifically, my intuitions are that if Jim does not compensate Frank, he has not acted unjustly.

Even if Jim desperately wanted to injure Frank and was busy conjuring up his own scheme to injure Frank, he still would not owe compensation as a matter of justice, because he did not cause the injury. This intuition or considered moral judgment can be easily generalized to cover a wide range of cases in which the beneficiary did not have a causal connection to the unjust injuring act. This pattern of considered moral judgments supports the claim that merely benefiting from an unjust act is not a sufficient condition to obligate payment on the basis of compensatory justice.[24] The underlying idea here is that a person owes a compensatory-justice-based debt only if she caused a rights-infringing harm.[25] I believe this causation is a justificationally primitive element in that it is not derived from more general moral principles, although others derive this requirement from the value of efficiency.[26] The causation requirement is independent from the issue of whether a compensatory-justice debt requires that the injurer be at fault.

One reply to this analysis is that under American law we require some innocent beneficiaries (e.g., recipients or innocent purchasers of stolen goods) to return the property to the original owner. Assuming that American law on this matter is justified, it seems to follow that under some circumstances innocent beneficiaries may be required to compensate injured persons.[27] It is argued that since young white males are sufficiently like innocent recipients of stolen goods, it is not unfair to make similar demands of them.

One problem with this reply is that the stolen goods analogy, even if it did provide some support for Principle #1, is less similar to the affirmative-action case than is Case #1. In the case of a stolen good, there is a physical thing that can be clearly identified and can be returned intact to the original owner. The innocent beneficiary does not necessarily invest effort or his resources into developing the stolen good. In Case #1, however, success in the tennis tournaments is not simply transferred from Frank to Jim. Frank's opportunity to compete was unjustly removed, but this does not, by itself, amount to a transfer of Frank's success to Jim. Jim must still put in great effort and invest some of his material resources in developing his ability before he can win the tennis championships and the accompanying prizes. This investment of time and effort constitutes a commitment of himself that can ground a desert claim or an entitlement claim to certain rewards. Similarly, in affirmative action, even if past unjust discrimination hampers the current success of blacks and women, this does not necessarily translate to success on behalf of a particular white male, who still needs to invest his resources and work hard in order to develop his abilities. This fact makes Case #1 (and cases like it) the better analogy to the case of affirmative action, hence, the accompanying intuitions are more relevant in assessing the program.

A second problem with this reply, however, is that the justification for American law in this area is better viewed as a consequentialist override of the innocent purchaser's rights for the purpose of eliminating a market in particular stolen goods, rather than as a result of distributive justice.

This can be seen in that the culpable wrongdoer and not the innocent beneficiary is the person who owes the victim compensation. If the culpable wrongdoer is not caught, then the innocent beneficiary is required to return the stolen goods and thereby to shoulder the accompanying financial loss. The innocent beneficiary, in many cases, is as morally innocent as the original owner, and perhaps more so if the original owner failed to take proper precautions against theft, and it is not clear why justice should favor the one over the other with regard to who should bear the loss that results from the culpable wrongdoer's actions. While the original owner may be owed a duty to be given compensation, that duty is distinguishable from the claim that she has a right to have her ownership in the actual good returned.

In contrast, the need to eliminate markets in stolen goods by encouraging purchasers to be very careful provides a compelling reason to favor the original owner. The consequentialist account also explains why there would be a statute of limitations on such claims, since this limitation prevents the problem of theft from greatly interfering with the free flow of products on the market, interference that might lead to wasteful research requirements into the historical origins of a marketplace good.

A white male is liable for compensation only if he actually consented to receive the benefits of past discrimination with adequate knowledge of their origin. Since many white males have not so consented, they may not be required to give up the protection of the duty to respect their interest or desert.

Approach #3: White Males Are Justifiably Required to Give the Duty They Are Owed So the Community Can Satisfy Its Debt of Compensatory Justice

Judith Jarvis Thomson argues that young white males do have a right to equal consideration, but that this right is overridden by the community's need to satisfy a debt of compensatory justice.[28] Her argument, which focuses solely on the case of women whose qualifications are equal to their white male competitors, proceeds as follows.

(P1) The community owes women a debt of compensation because of the community's history of discrimination.
(P2) The positions at state educational institutions are owned by the community and not (individually) by the young white males.
(P3) Affirmative-action programs involve the community setting aside the white male applicant's right to equal consideration.
(P4) If the community owes a debt to women because of past discrimination, and the community owns the relevant benefit, then the community is justified in setting aside the white male applicant's right to equal consideration to that benefit.
(C1) Hence, the community is justified in setting aside the white male applicant's right to equal consideration.
(C2) Hence, affirmative action is justified.

Let us grant (P1) through (P3). (P4) is the dubious premise. Note that (P4) differs from Principle #2.

Principle #2

Other things being equal, if a community owes compensation to certain persons, and if the costs of compensation cannot be assigned to the perpetrators of injustice, then each member of the community should bear an equal portion of those costs.[29]

Affirmative-action programs do not involve an even assignment of the costs of compensation. Rather, the costs are placed exclusively on those young white males who are competing for a position at particular state educational institutions. This assignment of costs is less egalitarian than a monetary payment that results from an even (or perhaps even a progressive) scheme of taxation. At the very least, there is good reason to be wary of any scheme that distributes the burdens in such an unequal manner.

The most important problem with the above argument is that (P4) is inapplicable because while the community owns the state educational institution, it does not own the right to equal consideration, hence, it may not set the right aside as a means of paying off its debt. Consideration of an analogous case should help illustrate this point.

Imagine that a community coercively and wrongly took a kidney from Jane for the purposes of a science experiment designed to benefit the whole community. After realizing the wrongful nature of its action, the community then offered to compensate Jane by replacing the lost kidney with the kidney of Richard, a young white male. The community chooses Richard's kidney because it is the kidney that most similarly resembles the one wrongly taken from Jane in tissue type, size, and condition. Richard objects on the ground that he has a right to his kidney. But using reasoning similar to Thomson's, the community claims that its debt of compensatory justice overrides this right (and also that Richard is not so innocent because he benefited, along with other community members, from the scientific experiment). Here our intuitions are that the community's preferred means of compensation is impermissible because the kidney is not the community's property to give away as it sees fit. Rather, Richard owns it, and absent his consent, it may not be taken from him.

Analogously, in affirmative action, the right to equal consideration (or the protection of the duty to respect one's interest or desert) is owned by the white male rather than being the community's property, hence, the community may not use it to pay off its debt of compensatory justice. Hence, (P4) is inapplicable because the community does not own the relevant benefit (i.e., the right to equal consideration).

There are likely to be two responses to this objection. First, it might be responded that the analogy fails because a lost student or teaching opportunity is much less of a sacrifice than the loss of a kidney. This difference in the level of sacrifice is what makes the community justified in requiring the former but not the latter sacrifice.

This difference in the level of sacrifice certainly seems to be correct. However, insofar as rights are viewed as trumps on considerations of utility or the interests of the community, it is not clear why the importance of the right is relevant to the question of whether the community may use it as a means of paying off its debt of compensation.[30] Insofar as we allow less important rights to be overridden by community-based concerns, we seem to be moving away from the view of rights (and of morality) as providing a bulwark against interference in a person's life. On this view of rights (and morality), persons are intrinsically valuable and thus ought to be granted certain spheres of noninterference that protect them from being used for the benefit of others.[31]

To the extent that one adopts consequentialist reasoning and rejects this picture, the defense of compensatory justice becomes less compelling, since consequentialist theories do not recognize compensatory justice as necessarily providing a sufficient moral reason for an action or a program. It should be noted that on some more recent consequentialist accounts, a more just state of affairs is a better consequence than a less just one, hence, concerns of compensatory justice are included in the overall consequentialist calculation.[32] This point is consistent with the above argument.[33]

Along these same lines, one might claim that the right to compensation conflicts with the right to equal consideration, and that the former right overrides the latter right, since the former is more important. However, it is a mistake to think that these two rights conflict. The right to compensation is best understood as the right to justly receive compensation in response to an unjust injury. This right does not include a right to whatever is necessary to place the person in qualitatively the same position she would have been had she lived in the possible world. If this were the content of the right, then the right to compensation would come into constant conflict with other specific rights to things or resources.

For example, imagine that Kim has her new Ford car stolen. If the right to compensation included whatever will put her in the position that she would have been in but for the unjust injury, then her right to compensation would conflict not only with the interests of the person who stole the car but also with the interests of all other persons who own new Ford cars, since the transfer of one of their cars to Kim would place her in the same position that she would have been in but for the theft. This constant and inevitable conflict of rights not only in this case but in countless similar cases would fail to respect the model of rights as preserving among innocent and competent persons a zone of noninterference against the attempt to pursue various societal goals, such as rectification of unjust injury.

Second, it might be responded that the analogy fails because unlike the case of the kidney, a person has no right to the educational or teaching spots at the university, and this can be seen in that no one would have a claim of a right being violated if the state eliminated the spot altogether. In other words, since the community owns the spot, it may use the spot as it sees fit, including as a means of compensation.

The problem with this response is that even if the educational spot is owned by the state, the right to equal consideration is not. To see this, imagine the case where the state, in response to the burdensome 40 percent effective tax rate on the income of an average American family, decides to no longer fund education at the university level. Assuming that there is no right to a college education, the state does not violate any person's rights to an education or to a teaching position. However, once the state decides to begin funding education at the university level again, it may not decide to give those benefits solely to male students, because women have a right to equal consideration. As a result, the right to equal consideration with regard to a particular benefit may exist, even if there is no right to the underlying benefit itself. This can be seen in that the former right may exist even where the latter right does not. That this right to equal consideration is owned by individuals rather than the state can be seen in that the state does not have the discretion to waive the right for any reason, as is true of (and perhaps an essential property of) a holder of a particular right.[34] Hence, the right to equal consideration is owned by particular individuals and not the state.

Since the right to equal consideration is privately owned, and since white males have in many cases not waived this right (and are not likely to if asked, given recent opinion surveys on racial and gender preferences), the community may not use the spot as it sees fit, and in particular it may not set it aside to pay its debt of compensation.

PART 4
Conclusion

In the context of state educational institutions, young white males are owed a duty to respect their interest or desert. Not all white males have waived this duty, since many have not performed the relevant types of culpable wrongdoing. Merely having benefited from an unjust injuring act or being a member of a community that owes a debt of compensation to racial minorities and women is not a sufficient ground to override the duty owed to the white male. Since the three most plausible attempts to provide a compensatory justice justification for strong affirmative-action programs at state educational institutions fail, I conclude that (1) is probably false.

> (1) Other things being equal, a state educational institution may choose to hire a less qualified candidate over a more qualified candidate, because the weight given to the race or gender of the less qualified candidate relates to the elimination of a debt of compensatory justice.

Hence, unless strong affirmative-action programs at state educational institutions can be justified by reference to some other value, such as the value of diversity, such programs ought to be eliminated. The same conclusion applies to the state's hiring practices and its giving out other state-financed benefits.

3

Uncertain Damages to Racial Minorities and Strong Affirmative Action

PART 1
The Hypothetical Imperative to Distribute Resources in a Just Manner

Unlike the state, private parties have the right to hire and give resources to whomever they want. I will leave aside whether this is the result of property rights, freedom of association, John Stuart Mill's harm principle, or some other moral element. Some seemingly private institutions may have much less discretion insofar as they are quasi-governmental entities given the state protection of their monopoly (e.g., the United States Postal Service), however, they are not very numerous and I shall not discuss them. My interest in this chapter is not whether private institutions have a right to implement strong affirmative-action programs but whether they ought to do so on the basis of compensatory justice; I shall argue that they ought not. My background assumptions here are that an individual or a group sometimes has a right to do a wrongful action or an action whose motivation rests on an error in moral reasoning, and that paying compensation to individuals to whom compensation is not owed sometimes fits into the second category.[1] This need not make such an action wrongful, unless one thinks, as I do not, that there is a duty to act on the basis of correct moral reasoning.

Even if one thinks that it is not in itself wrongful to act on the basis of incorrect moral reasoning, there can still be hypothetical imperatives against such acts. Consider a generous man who thinks that he is benefiting a neighbor by giving him cash where the neighbor is a closet drug addict who uses the money to buy drugs that permanently damage him. The generous man may not be acting wrongfully, insofar as he violates no perfect or imperfect duty, but he may frustrate his own purpose, which is to benefit the neighbor. Such an act may violate the benefactor's own hypothetical imperative, and while not wrongful, such violations are often bad insofar as they set back the benefactor's interests. If compensatory justice does not support strong affirmative action, and I argue for this below, then private parties violate hypothetical imperatives if they implement such programs on behalf of compensatory justice.

Private employers and other institutions have a number of motivations by which to institute a strong affirmative-action program. They might be motivated to do so on the basis of backward-looking goals, such as compensatory justice, or forward-looking goals, such as diversity. The last goal is usually a means by which historically oppressed minority groups are given benefits such as role models, mentors, or a sufficient number of members so that the members do not feel isolated or that they are mere tokens. Also, promoting racial or sex diversity is sometimes a way in which an institution or employer brings about a broad array of opinions. Upon examination, the backward- and forward-looking motivations often tend to be either an attempt to satisfy a job qualification or an attempt to achieve just compensation for members of injured groups. For example, many of these goals are attempts to determine qualifications (e.g., opinion diversity) rather than attempts to promote members of historically disadvantaged groups. However, in cases in which the attempt is not aimed at satisfying a job qualification but another goal (e.g., role models and equal opportunity), the underlying motivation is often compensatory. This is because the notion that steps should be taken to provide role models or equal opportunity often depends on the idea that such treatment is a permissible, if not required, response to past injustices. The issue gets more complex where such a program is a job qualification (because it is closely tied to an employer's job-related preference) in virtue of its compensatory function. Here the issue can again be recast in terms of whether the employer's having this goal violates a hypothetical imperative.

It should also be noted that this argument is independent of the argument in the previous chapter. The previous chapter focused on who ought to pay the debt of compensatory justice, whereas this chapter focuses on whether we have sufficient knowledge to assess whether there is such a debt and if so how large it is.

PART 2
Compensatory Justice and the Assessment of Damages

An act of strong affirmative action involves giving preference to minority and women candidates who are less qualified than others, usually with regard to a job, an educational opportunity, or some other benefit. A widely cited moral justification for strong affirmative action is the value of compensatory justice. I limit my discussion to state institutions to screen out concerns for private property rights and freedom of association, however, it should be noted that my argument does have implications for private institutions in that they aim to provide just compensation to historically oppressed groups.

In this chapter, I argue that we should adopt the following principle with regard to compensatory justice.

(1) If an unjust act benefits an innocent person and there is no reasonable way to assess the amount of the damages to the victim, then compensatory justice does not require that the innocent beneficiary pay compensation for those damages.

I further argue that with regard to historical injustices to racial minorities, there is no reasonable way to assess the amount of harm done to current racial minorities. As a result, I conclude that compensatory justice does not require that innocent white male candidates pay compensation for damages that have resulted from past unjust acts.

PART 3
Compensatory Justice and Inadequate Knowledge of Damages

Compensatory justice aims at eliminating or rectifying unjustifiable gains and losses. Since the purpose of the compensatory-justice justification is to place the injured person in the qualitatively same position she would have been in but for the unjust injurious act, the justification requires that we be able to determine the amount of compensation that is necessary to place her in this position. Cases in which the victim is unable to quantify her damages create a risk that any payment will overcompensate or undercompensate the victim, thereby putting her in a different position than she would have been in but for the token harm. In general, it seems preferable that the morally guilty injuring party should bear the risk of overcompensating the victim, because the injuring party is morally guilty in that he performed the culpable wrongdoing[2] that created the need for compensation. In the context of strong affirmative action, however, a problem arises, since there are no morally guilty parties who can be asked to pay compensation.

The best-qualified white male candidate (this fact about relative qualification follows from the definition of strong affirmative action), insofar as he is passed up for lesser-qualified racial minorities, is asked to sacrifice a duty that is normally owed to him. This duty is grounded in a white male's greater desert and greater educational interests. As the hampering of the white male's candidacy increases, so too does the wrongfulness of the overriding of this duty.

Jules Coleman challenges the claim that compensatory justice demands that the morally guilty injurer be the source of compensation. He argues that compensatory justice requires the removal of unjust gains and losses but does not require that these goals be pursued through the transfer of resources from the injuring party to the party that suffered the harm,[3] although he acknowledges that other moral reasons might warrant such a demand.

Coleman gives three main arguments for his position. First, he argues, the right of the innocent victim to compensation does not entail a duty on behalf of the injurer, even if he is morally guilty, to pay the compensation. Coleman uses this example to illustrate his point.

> [I]f X borrows a sum of money from Y with the understanding that he will repay it, Y has a valid claim against X for that sum. Should Z intervene and reimburse Y for X, there are no grounds upon which Y could protest that he has done an injustice.[4]

What this example shows, according to Coleman, is that the right to compensation (or duty to be compensated) does not entail a duty in the injuring agent to pay that compensation. Coleman's argument seems to be that this right (or claim) differs from an *in personam* claim-right (a right for which there is a correlative duty against a particular person), since implicit in the latter right is a prima facie duty on behalf of a specific person to perform (or omit to perform) an act.

Second, he argues that, since the rights violator may not gain anything from her act or her gain may be unrelated to the harm the victim incurs, compensatory justice does not require that the violator's gain be used to offset the victim's loss.[5] For example, a batterer who severely beats a person while robbing her might not gain any money, satisfaction, or political liberty from his act.[6] Since the rights violator need not gain from the victim or his gain may be unrelated to the victim's injury, Coleman concludes that compensatory justice does not require that the wrongdoer compensate the victim for her losses.

Third, Coleman argues that retributivism does not justify requiring compensation from those at fault, since retributivism grounds liability on moral guilt, and fault often does not track moral guilt.[7]

There are two points to be made about Coleman's theory. First, on some accounts of rights, all rights are either negative (i.e., rights against certain acts of commission by other persons) or contractually incurred. On one version of this account, if an innocent person is required to pay part of the compensation costs for the injured party and she has not contractually incurred this obligation, then her property rights to her wealth are violated.[8] Coleman might agree with this and assert that in cases in which the injurer does not compensate the victim, compensatory justice claims either may not be satisfied or may be satisfied by means that violate a person's property rights. If compensatory justice is viewed as including within its scope negative property rights, and if these rights are given great weight, then we end up requiring those at fault (or at least a pool of them) to compensate victims. Hence, we end up accepting (2).

> (2) Compensatory justice requires person A to compensate person B only if either A harmed B or A contracted to compensate B.

Second, if Coleman is correct in arguing that compensatory justice does not address the issue of who should pay compensation, then compensatory justice will not by itself support placing liability on white males who in the context of strong affirmative action are more qualified than their non-white male competitors. Rather, compensatory justice will then result in there being a moral reason to provide compensation to certain racial minorities, but it will not address the issue of who should provide the compensation. Since essential to strong affirmative action is the taking of something from the best-qualified white male, compensatory justice, on Coleman's account, would therefore be unable to provide a prima facie case for such programs.

Since innocent beneficiaries of an unjust act are often as morally innocent as the injured party, an expansive view of compensatory justice (i.e., where it contains negative and heavily weighted property rights within its scope) does not permit us to place the risk of improper compensation on the innocent beneficiary. This can be seen in the following thought experiment.

> A steals a box from owner B and gives it to her, A's, granddaughter, C. C does not know and could not have discovered the unjust origin of this box. A then dies. One year later, C accidentally destroys the box in a car accident. A, B, and C all have no idea of the box's value, and cannot discover, even with due diligence, its value.

C does not owe B compensation, because there does not seem to be any justice-related reason to put the risk of overcompensation on her rather than putting the risk of undercompensation on B. This is because concerns relating to desert, fairness, and equality do not distinguish B and C. And any liability that relates to B's property right does not fall on C's shoulders, since she was neither at fault nor morally guilty with regard to the violation of this right.

This type of thought experiment is easily generalized to reflect a wide range of cases, all of which produce similar intuitions. Hence, we should adopt the following principle.

(3) Where an unjust act benefits a faultless and morally innocent person and there is no reasonable way to assess the amount of the damages, compensatory justice does not permit us to require that the innocent beneficiary pay damages.

Young white males are morally innocent parties with regard to the unjust injuring acts done to blacks and Hispanics. This can be seen in that many white males have not culpably interfered with the civil rights of racial minorities. Nor have many white males knowingly accepted the benefits of past unjust actions (e.g., the competitive advantage and extra self-esteem). This is true in part because some of the benefits are given to white males in childhood, that is, before informed consent can be given, and in part because one cannot realistically reject the intangible and often unnoticeable advantages that accompany one's being a white male. A substantial number of white males have even worked to reverse the effects of past discrimination, although omitting to do so would probably not be a sufficient moral reason for owing compensation.

Where the innocent beneficiary receives intangible assets such as increased opportunity (e.g., an enhanced ability to compete for jobs),[9] or psychological benefits such as enhanced self-esteem,[10] the risks of overcompensating and undercompensating the victim emerge. Hence, if we cannot assess the value of the non-white males' losses, then compensatory justice does not require that innocent white males pay compensation.

PART 4
We Do Not Have Adequate Knowledge of the Amount of Compensable Injury to Current Members of Some Racial Minority Groups

The Cumulative Case

If the number, complexity, and interplay of the factors having to do with injuries to members of some racial minority groups are so great that we cannot reasonably estimate the overall injury, then strong affirmative-action programs cannot be justified on the basis of compensatory justice. I will provide three general problems that illustrate the difficulty of this estimation.

Problem #1: Who Is Injured?

The issue of whether African Americans have been harmed by historical injustices such as slavery can be understood to be equivalent to asking whether the descendants of slaves would have suffered the same token harm in the relevant comparison world where slavery is not instituted.[11] The focus on token harms allows us to escape the notion that slavery may have had a net beneficial effect on the descendants of slaves by giving them access to economic opportunity and liberty that they would otherwise not have had access to.[12] The claim to compensation rests not on the net effects of slavery but rather on slavery's having produced token harms to the descendants of slaves. The problem is that some unjust injuring acts, particularly acts of slavery, led to intercourse and the later creation of the ancestors of many members of minority groups.[13] Hence, there is no possible world in which these individuals exist and in which the injustice (e.g., slavery) did not occur. As a result, the counterfactual test does not allow us to understand, let alone measure, the existence of a compensable injury to these persons.[14] For simplicity, I have chosen to focus on slavery. However, a similar argument can be made with regard to Native Americans, interned Japanese Americans, etc., since unjust treatment affected the mate selection and reproductive choices of members of these groups.

An objector might agree that a descendant of slaves may not have existed in the relevant possible world and hence cannot legitimately claim to have been harmed in the actual world. Still, the objector might claim, in the actual world white males have benefited from past injustices (e.g., by gaining unwarranted self-esteem or an unfair competitive advantage), and thus compensatory justice requires that these benefits be returned. However, even if white males have benefited from these past unjust acts, compensatory justice does not require that the unjust gains be transferred from them to uninjured parties. Such a move would, at most, transfer the injustice in the distribution of unjust benefits from one innocent party to another, rather than rectifying the injustice.

One might argue that the slaves are owed compensation and that after death their moral claims to it are transferred to their inheritors through either a will or more likely through implicit inheritance practices.[15] I am assuming here that among the essential elements of property rights is the right of the original property owner to give away her property and the right of the inheritor to receive the property, and that property rights entail prima facie moral duties of noninterference. According to this account, if the enslaved person had not been enslaved in the relevantly similar possible world, and if the slave's inheritors are the rightful owners of the slave's property, and if the inheritors of the slave's property are likely her descendants, then compensatory justice supports compensation being owed to the slave's descendants.

A different but related account is that the slave retains her moral claim to compensation, even after death, and that this claim survives her death. On this account, the descendants never own the claim to compensation but merely assert it on behalf of the deceased slaves in the same way in which an estate's trustee may claim (both morally and legally) the right to recover money owed to the deceased after she dies. On this account, the descendants merely assert the rights of the deceased slaves, and the compensation is owed to the slaves themselves. And given that the trustees of the slaves' estates are probably their descendants, the descendants may choose to distribute the money to themselves. This account rests on the assumption that a person may have a moral claim in receiving just compensation even after her death.

Note that neither account rests on the claim that the current descendants of slaves were harmed by slavery, and thus both accounts escape concerns that relate to their nonexistence in the relevant possible world.

In the case of the descendants, if failure to pay compensation to the slave's descendants sets back the descendants' interest in being given their rightful inheritance or the slave's interest in being treated in a just manner, then the failure may be an unjust omission that grounds a legitimate claim to compensation. However, even on this inheritance model, we would need to identify the injuring agents and the injuring acts in order to identify the amount of inheritance that is owed. I now turn to this task.

Problem #2: Who Is the Unjust Injuring Agent? What Is the Unjust Injuring Act?

For determining the amount of compensation owed to racial minorities, the identity of the injuring party matters greatly.

In general, persons do not owe compensation for unjust injuring acts done by private individuals. For example, if a drunken and racist white male beats up a young Mexican-American male, then this does not give rise to a legitimate claim of compensation against other white males. In the case of racial minorities, many of the injuring acts were done by private white males with no coordination or encouragement by government at any level, hence, these injuries or their effects cannot ground a claim of compensation against innocent white males.

Where government officials are involved, the identity of the official is important in determining which citizens owe compensation. For example, where a Georgia state official participates in an unjust injuring act (e.g., he acts to disenfranchise blacks in his community), this particular act does not give rise to a legitimate claim for compensation from the citizens of Connecticut. In the case where government officials are involved in the unjust injuring act, a white male owes compensation only if he lives in the jurisdiction of that official, so that any debt is incurred by the white male's "agent," and only if the official was acting in his official capacity. Normally we do not hold citizens liable when government officials perform wrongdoings that are completely outside the scope of their official capacity.

It might be objected that all American citizens owe compensation, since their agent, the federal government, omitted to intervene to prevent private persons and state and local officials from committing unjust acts. Under American law, an omission by itself does not give rise to compensatory liability unless the victim was owed a special duty. In American criminal law, a mere omission in the absence of a special duty to the injured party will not give rise to criminal liability.[16] A similar rule applies to tort suits.[17] An analogous doctrine should be seen to apply to the context of morality, that is, if one person merely omits to help a second person and if the first person has no special duty to the second, then, other things being equal, the first person does not owe compensation to the second. There are several reasons behind this moral doctrine.

First, in the absence of this doctrine, we would constantly owe compensation to various persons we could have but did not help protect. Proper consideration of our own projects and pleasures would threaten to make the moral demand of compensation either negligible, because the moral value of our projects would always outweigh it, or impermissibly demanding, requiring us to sacrifice a large portion of our projects and pleasures. It is possible, however, that a middle ground can be reached that would escape these twin dangers.

Second, insofar as causation is a necessary condition for compensatory liability, and insofar as omissions are not events or at least not the type of event that can function as a cause, an omission (e.g., the federal government's omitting to prevent state and private parties from violating persons' rights) will not meet a necessary condition for compensatory liability.

Third, our intuitions do not support compensation in cases where no special duty exists. Consider the following example.

> A woman comes upon an infant drowning face down in a puddle of water. The woman, a successful attorney in an expensive suit, has no special relation to the infant and does nothing, since she does not want to lose valuable time at the office. The infant dies four minutes later.

Now we might all agree that this woman is callous and that her omission is wrong. But as a moral matter, does she owe compensation to the infant's estate or to the infant's parents? My intuitions are that she does not, or at the very least it is not clear that she does. And the case gets clearer the more the intervention requires the bystander to invest effort or income, or to sacrifice important interests. The moral difference between acting and omission may relate to the difference between the stringency of negative and positive duties or to the difference between the stringency of negative and positive rights, although a defense of this claim is beyond the scope of this chapter.

The objector might claim that the federal government has a special duty to American citizens to protect their basic moral rights. Hence, the federal government's historical failure to protect the basic rights of some racial minorities grounds a legitimate claim to compensation on behalf of their descendants. The idea behind this objection is that the federal government's special duty rests on whatever justification warrants the federal government's authority. This duty does not follow immediately from the federal government's authority, since the authority may be limited in that it extends only to a specific list of enumerated powers, none of which includes the open-ended power to protect basic rights. However, if one accepts (which I do not) the more modern view of federal authority as justifiably including, within the individual-rights based constraints set forth in the Constitution, the power to prevent any violation of basic rights, then the objection succeeds.

Even if we grant this objection, the problems multiply when we try to separate out the percentage of injury that resulted from wrongful omissions by the federal government. Such a task seems incredibly complex and likely to block any reasonable estimation of the degree of injury that is capable of warranting compensation. Such a task increases still further in complexity when we try to determine the degree to which this injury resulted from interference with counterfactual inheritance practices.

A related problem is that of identifying the injuring act. Was it the maintenance and enforcement of slavery? Later acts of segregation? Before we can know whom the injuring party is, we have to know what the injuring act is. What is needed is a specification capable of allowing us to see if the identity of the act and the agent give rise to a duty to pay compensation among innocent white male applicants. This problem is especially noticeable in the context of strong affirmative-action programs toward non-blacks. For example, Mexican Americans, including recent immigrants, get a large break toward a vast array of academic programs.[18]

We do not have a clear idea of the acts and agents that give rise to the pattern of compensable injury. Without such a clear idea, requiring a certain amount of compensation by innocent white males relies on mere guesswork.

Problem #3: What Is the Degree of Injury to Racial Minorities?

Compensation is designed to rectify only those disadvantages that result from unjust injuring acts or the effects of those acts, where the injured party cannot reasonably have ameliorated the effects. Disadvantages that accompany group differences in genetics and sociocultural values do not warrant compensation, since these factors are not the direct result of past or present unjust acts. In order to assess the amount of compensation owed, we have to discount the effects of these factors in producing various inequalities between groups. Since such discounting is an extraordinarily complex task, it seems as though we probably cannot disentangle the effects of such factors.

In calculating the amount of compensation owed, problems arise in the setting of the baseline. Often it is assumed that but for discrimination, there would be an equal distribution of members of the different groups in various areas of employment. For example, it is often assumed that but for discrimination there would be an equal number of whites, African Americans, and Asian Americans in particular fields, such as medicine, law, teaching, etc. The notion underlying this assumption is that no group has a strongly held advantage in any field that cannot be traced back, however far, to discrimination. This notion is questionable, but without this baseline the calculation of compensation becomes extraordinarily difficult. For example, if groups differ with regard to the distribution of IQ (the measure of intelligence), and if a large portion of the IQ is genetic,[19] then there may be a cognitive advantage for some groups, such as Russian-Jewish immigrants[20] and some Asian-American groups.[21]

In addition, there may be differences in the sociocultural beliefs, attitudes, and values between different groups. While not genetic, these are deeply embedded factors that may have large effects on the success of members of those groups in certain fields.[22] Given the existence of a pattern of unequal distributions of IQ and sociocultural factors across different countries, it is doubtful that these effects can accurately be explained solely in terms of American discrimination.

Some destructive behavior that is not the result of discrimination may produce inequalities between groups. For example, in the mid-1990s blacks had nearly a 70 percent out-of-wedlock birth rate.[23] Since out-of-wedlock birth is associated with many destructive behaviors (e.g., crime), attitudes and activity leading to out-of-wedlock births have harmful effects on members of the black community. Blacks also commit a disproportionately large number of violent crimes. They constitute approximately 50 percent to 60 percent of the arrests for murder, about 50 percent of the arrests for rape, and close to 60 percent of the arrests for robbery.[24] Since these arrest rates match the frequency distribution of victims' reports, they do not appear to reflect a bias in arrests.[25] Out-of-wedlock births and violent crimes are in general voluntary acts for which moral responsibility rests on the agent who performs those acts. When such acts form a general pattern in the black community, they produce an unequal distribution of income and wealth when compared to other racial groups. The effects of this destructive behavior should be disentangled from those injuries that justify a compensatory debt. But disentangling these factors is a daunting task.

In determining the amount of compensation owed, we normally require that the injured party make a good-faith effort to minimize her losses. Where such an attempt is not made, we lower the estimate of compensation owed.

For example, in law, a person injured in a car accident, who can no longer perform her original job, receives damages for lost wages but not for wages that could have been obtained through having a different job within the post-accident skills of the injured party. Failure to take such a job is relevant in determining the amount that the accident victim is entitled to. Similarly, with regard to members of a victimized group, compensation is not owed where the members have, to a large degree, not taken active steps to ameliorate the effects of an unjust injuring act. To the extent that the above patterns of behavior occur, many members of some racial minority groups may not have made attempts at amelioration.

One last concern is that the program itself not injure the racial minorities that it is trying to help. Strong affirmative-action programs are justified as compensation only if we know (or reasonably believe) that the programs' injurious effects do not exist or are overridden by the program's positive effects. However, the effects of strong affirmative action are controversial, with some authors claiming that these programs actually hurt the targeted groups. For example, some authors have argued that strong affirmative-action programs hurt blacks by encouraging discriminatory attitudes in whites,[26] by damaging individual blacks' self-confidence,[27] by placing blacks in schools where they are at a competitive disadvantage, thereby significantly increasing the chance that they will fail,[28] and by lowering competence and efficiency, which is especially likely to hurt the most vulnerable groups in society, groups in which blacks are overrepresented.[29]

Given the multitude of these causal factors and the complex interplay between them, it seems that we cannot currently gain a reasonable measurement of the amount of compensable damage that has resulted from past unjust acts.

PART 5
Conclusion

We should adopt the following principle with regard to compensatory justice.

(1) If an unjust act benefits an innocent person and there is no reasonable way to assess the amount of the damages to the victim, then compensatory justice does not require that the innocent beneficiary pay compensation for those damages.

We cannot reasonably assess the amount of damages to current racial minorities resulting from past discriminatory acts. Problems arise in determining the identity of the injured parties, the identity of the injuring agents and injuring acts (and omissions), and the degree of injury that directly resulted from these acts (and omissions). Since such compensable damages cannot be accurately estimated, and since white male applicants are innocent beneficiaries of past discriminatory acts, the value of compensatory justice does not justify strong affirmative-action programs.

SECTION 4

Reparations for Slavery

4

The Inheritance-Based Claim to Reparations

The case for reparations for slavery is somewhat independent of the case for strong affirmative-action programs. This is because state payment of money to its victims or their descendants may rest on a more just system for distributing the burdens of this debt than does a strong affirmative-action program. In particular, the former programs need not place the full weight of compensation on a narrow class such as the most qualified applicants who are also white males. That the state would owe compensation for the unjust actions of its agents is not surprising. We often think that principals who direct their agents to intentionally harm others may owe compensation. For example, a head of a Mafia family who directs his employee to break the leg of a union leader intuitively seems to owe compensation to that leader, especially where the employee is unable to do so. In addition, the relation between the state and individual citizens is far more coercive than the relationship between most principals and agents, hence, the case for state compensation strengthens considerably. In addition, the epistemic problems with reparations might be initially thought to be less severe. In the context of reparations, we can use techniques for estimating the compensation owed to slaves that are similar to the techniques used in tort law to assess the compensation owed for workplace injuries, lost income, pain and suffering, and death. Thus we shall now investigate whether slavery grounds a legitimate claim in the descendants of American slaves to compensation against the state.

PART 1
Introduction

The notion that the current descendants of slaves are owed compensation for slavery is one that receives widespread discussion and support. For example, in 1989, Representative John Conyers of Michigan proposed legislation that would create a commission to explore the effects of slavery on both African Americans and the United States. More recently, Randall Robinson, in *The Debt: What America Owes to Blacks,* argued that an important step toward healing racial division and helping poor African Americans is to compensate blacks for slavery.[1] Also, a well-known group of civil rights and class-action attorneys, including Harvard law professor Charles Ogletree and Johnnie Cochran, is putting together a lawsuit seeking reparations for the descendants of slaves.[2] The debt on some estimates involves trillions of dollars.[3] In this chapter, I argue that the descendants of slaves were not harmed by slavery, since they owe their existence to slavery. I then recognize that they may have a claim to compensation based on their having inherited their ancestors' (i.e., the slaves') claim to compensation. I argue that the inheritance-based claim is defeated by a number of concerns, particularly doubt surrounding the existence and amount of this inheritance-based claim, concerns about offsets (sums that must be subtracted from compensation), and problems concerning the identity of any contemporary public or private entity that owes compensation. Note that in this chapter I will not discuss harms that were not the result of enslavement, hence, I set aside some of the claims put forth on behalf of current African Americans.

PART 2
Slavery Did Not Harm the Descendants of Slaves

The compensatory-justice justification of reparations involves an attempt to rectify a compensable injury that resulted from slavery. This requires a comparison of the actual world in which the injured party lives to a relevantly similar possible world in which this party lives but where the unjust injuring act never occurred in order to identify the degree of harm brought about by the unjust injurious act. Identifying the effects of this act allows us to estimate the amount of compensation owed to certain racial minorities (e.g., individual African Americans). The problem is that some unjust injuring acts, particularly acts of slavery, led to intercourse and the later creation of the ancestors of many members of minority groups. Hence, among the relevant possible worlds, there is no case in which these individuals exist and in which the injustice (e.g., slavery) did not occur. As a result, the counterfactual test does not allow us to measure or even understand the existence of a compensable injury to these persons.[4]

Compensatory Justice and Token Harms

Compensatory justice generally relies on a comparison of the actual world in which the injured party lives to a relevantly similar possible world in which this party lives but where the unjust injuring act never occurred. Just compensation places the person in qualitatively the same position she would have been had she lived in the possible world. As discussed in chapter 2, this test for harm needs to be tightened up, however, in order to take into account token harm. This was illustrated by the case of the two delinquent boys who plan to push a woman in front of an oncoming truck. So the issue becomes whether the descendants of slaves would have suffered the same token harm in the relevant comparison world where slavery is not instituted.

The focus on token harms allows us to escape the following sort of argument against compensation for slavery.

> If we could make sense of the effects of slavery on the descendants of slaves, we cannot be sure that the effects are harmful. Slavery may have had a net positive effect on the descendants by giving them access to advanced technology and greater wealth they would otherwise not have had access to. If we measure the comparative positions of current African Americans and current Africans in terms of income, civil rights, education, or economic opportunity, slavery would have produced a net benefit for the descendants of slaves, and hence it does not support compensation.[5]

The problem with this argument is that it assumes that the claim to compensation rests on the *net effects* of slavery rather than on slavery's having produced *token harms* to the descendants of slaves. Consider the following analogy. Using a bat, Alice intentionally shatters Betty's arm. As a result, Betty refocuses her efforts from sports to academics, eventually leading to a flourishing medical career. If it has not yet been paid, it intuitively seems that Alice still owes Betty compensation, even though the attack, on the whole, benefited Betty.[6]

An Analogy: The Wrongful Refusal to Have an Abortion

Joel Feinberg argues that there are cases where a wrongdoing can be recognized even where the counterfactual test is unusable.[7] Perhaps his approach can be used to explain how the descendants of slaves can be said to have a compensable injury as a result of the mistreatment of their ancestors.

Feinberg asserts that there are cases in which a woman should have aborted her fetus, where the fetus is defective and likely to live in pain, because it would have been better for the baby not to have existed than for it to have been born. He argues that in cases like these the baby is not harmed, because the actual world in which the baby exists cannot be compared to the most similar possible world in which the woman aborted the fetus, because the baby never existed in that world. But the infant, on his analysis, has been wronged, because the refusal to have an abortion produced a baby without its birth rights, which are welfare rights that protect (in most people) interests that are necessary to the fulfillment of other more ultimate interests, no matter what they turn out to be.

To see why Feinberg's account fails to support the notion that the wrongdoing of slavery produces a compensable injury in the descendants of slaves, we need to consider the two main accounts of wrongdoing.

On one account of wrongdoing, one person wrongs a second person just in case the first sets back a legitimate interest of the second.[8] This account might have to be modified to require that the agent be culpable for her act. On this account, every wrongdoing is a harming. Since, by hypothesis, the infant is not harmed, it follows that the infant is not wronged. An analogous argument applies to the alleged wronging of the descendants of slaves.

On a second account of wrongdoing, one person wrongs a second person just in case the first performs a prima facie morally impermissible act (or omission) that fails to satisfy a duty owed to the second. This account might also have to be modified to require that the agent be culpable for her act. Underlying this account is the notion that there is a duty not to bring suffering persons into existence, since the presence of this suffering would be bad for these persons, and since the absence of this suffering is neutral if not good (even though there is nobody to experience the absence).[9] This comparison involves not a comparison of two possible states of the person (i.e., a state where she exists and one where she does not) but rather a comparison of two states of affairs (i.e., one with the suffering person and one without her). Hence, on this account, the baby is wronged but not harmed by the person who brought about the state of affairs, even though the opposite state of affairs would not have benefited the nonexistent baby.

However, even if the state of affairs in which a person suffers is inferior to a state of affairs in which she does not exist, this inferiority does not ground a legitimate claim of compensation on behalf of the suffering person. And even if the second account can get around this objection, we still cannot say that the descendants of slaves were wronged but not harmed by slavery. On the second account, a baby may be wronged if it would have been preferable for it not to have existed at all than for it to have existed with its defects. The same cannot be said for the descendants of slaves, many of whom are flourishing, hence, the analogy falls apart.

So the descendants of slaves are not owed compensation on the basis of slavery being a harmless wrongdoing.

An Attempt to Show that the Descendants of Slaves Exist in the Relevant Possible World

One objection is that contrary to my initial argument, the same African Americans exist in both the relevant possible world and the actual world. Since they are better off in the former world, slavery gives rise to a legitimate claim of compensation on behalf of current African Americans.[10] The idea underlying this objection is that since the relevant possible world contains the same African Americans as the actual world, it is more similar to the actual world than possible worlds that do not have these persons, hence, is the appropriate baseline for comparison. In the relevant possible world, the objection goes, the same African Americans exist because the persons who were slaves in the actual world but not the relevant possible world voluntarily came to America and chose to reproduce with the same persons that they reproduced with in the actual world.

The purpose of the relevant counterfactual is to determine those effects that result from the injuring act. To do so, the relevant possible world should include the condition of a person wrongfully injured in the actual world in the most similar world in which the injuring act did not occur. Since we use the differences between the actual world and the relevant possible world as a measure of the effects of the unjust wrongdoing, the relevant possible world must be identical to the actual world up until the time of the injuring act. Hence, we determine the conditions under the relevant possible world by assuming that the conditions in it are (pretty much) identical with those in the actual world up until the time of the injury and then envisioning the most probable outcome if the injuring act had not occurred. Here an outcome is probable relative to the evidence that we currently have.

The above objection, however, holds fixed many significant post-injury acts and conditions, such as acts of intercourse between specific persons and the movement of specific Africans to America. These significant post-injury acts can plausibly be held fixed only if the pre-injury conditions in the relevant possible world differ from conditions in the pre-injury actual world. But this difference would defeat the purpose of the counterfactual, which is to identify those effects of the unjust wrongdoing.[11] An example may help illustrate the error. The objector may claim that in the relevant possible world, white slave traders would not have coerced (and may have paid) the persons who were slaves in the actual world but not the relevant possible world to come to America, thereby allowing for the movement of the same Africans to America. This arrangement seems plausible though only if vast economic changes and changes in the widely accepted beliefs occurred in the period immediately preceding the American slave trade. But since in any usable world these changes would predate American enslavement, they must be left out of the relevant possible world. Hence, in the relevant possible world, some of the Africans may not have met in America and reproduced, as they did in the actual world, hence, the relevant possible world would not contain the same persons as the actual world. Here I am assuming that the identity of a person's parents is an essential property of her. The objector might reply that my response is a problem for any counterfactual in which enslavement does not occur. However, if this is correct, then what this shows is that in enslavement, there is no plausible account of the relevant counterfactual that can be used to justify a claim for compensation.

Counterintuitive Results of This Model of Harm

One concern with the model of harm that I adopt in this section is that it has some counterintuitive implications. On this model, a benefit (or harm) is a promotion (or setback) of a person's particular interest compared to a counterfactual baseline.[12] Depending on the account one adopts, this baseline is a function of the person's likely or morally permissible degree of satisfaction with regard to that particular interest. A benefit (or harm) on this account relates to the promotion (or setback) of a particular interest relative to the baseline, and since a given act can affect different interests in different ways, it can produce both a benefit and a harm.

One counterintuitive result of this model is that parents do not benefit a person by conceiving her. This is because there is no possible world in which she exists and is not conceived by them. Yet persons have a strong sense of gratitude toward their parents, and this emotional fact suggests that the parents did confer a benefit. The strong sense of gratitude may be explained by the parent's efforts toward their child after birth. However, in the case of a parent who gave a child up for adoption, such an explanation will not work. I suggest that the sense of gratitude is mistaken (or at least the judgment that generates it is), although positing such a widespread error does provide some reason to doubt my account.[13]

My claim is that since present-day persons would not have existed if their parents had not conceived them, these individuals cannot benefit from conception. An objector might claim that this does not follow.[14] He might argue that given that a person X actually exists, we can meaningfully ask "How much value-for-X does this counterfactual world have?" even if X does not exist in that world. If the world is one in which X's parents did not conceive her, then it seems that the world has zero value for her. It would then follow that if X's life is actually worth living, then she was benefited. There are two things to note about this objection. First, if successful, it does not weaken my argument, since most descendants of slaves have lives worth living and thus were benefited by slavery. Second, this objection assumes that a world in which a person does not exist can have *value for her*. This is an error if a thing must exist in order to be a subject of properties.[15]

Another counterintuitive result is that the same treatment can be a benefit to one person and a harm to another, since it may promote the interest of the first while setting back the interest of the second.[16] However, this does not seem problematic once we recognize that a benefit or harm is a function of the effect on a person, and that the same act may have different effects on different people (or even on the same person). So, for example, making a job offer to one person may benefit her given her desperate state and may offend another given her career success.[17]

Objections to This Model of Harm

An objector might challenge my reasoning on the grounds that either the counterfactual analysis does not determine whether slavery is harmful or that it does and I have applied it incorrectly.

An objector might make the following argument. That a person exists in the appropriate possible world (e.g., a world close to our own, except that it has no slavery) may be a presupposition of her having been harmed by slavery in the real world. But if the presupposition fails, it does not follow that the person has not been harmed. What follows is that we cannot say that she has been harmed and cannot say that she has not been harmed. However, harm is a comparative notion. A person is harmed by an event only if she in some sense would have been worse off than she would have been had this event not occurred. Hence, where a person does not exist in the appropriate possible world relative to slavery, it follows that she is not harmed by it.

Even if harm is a comparative notion, the objector might point out that slavery does not consist of the act of initial enslavement alone. Rather, it consists of an extremely large number of particular acts (and omissions) whereby slavery is maintained. For example, consider where a person lives in slavery for n days and where slavery is abolished the next day. Consider the slave's final day in slavery (i.e., the nth day). If he were freed on that day, then he would live that day in America as a free man. The harm done to him on that day by the acts that maintain slavery is to be measured relative to a baseline (i.e., his living that day in America as a free man). The acts that maintain slavery also harm his descendants if they would have been better off had the slave been freed that day. This last point is plausible only up to the point where the first post-slavery generation is created.[18] Before the point of creation, if the slave had been freed, then in some, if not many, cases the slave would have reproduced with different persons or done so at a different time, thus using different genetic material, and this would have produced a different line of descendants. My assumption here is that a person's parents (i.e., her causal origin) and genetics (i.e., structural blueprint) are essential features of her. This alone prevents the descendants from having a compensatory claim relating some, if not most, of the time during which generations of their ancestors were enslaved. Also, note that if the maintenance of slavery did not produce a token harm for the slave's descendants, then no claim to compensation is generated. To see this, consider that an ex-slave might have been killed or disabled as a result of his participation as a soldier in the Civil War.

For the last generation of slaves during the period of time following reproduction, the acts that maintained slavery may well have harmed the slaves' descendants. This alone does not ground a claim to compensation, since such a claim requires both a harm and an infringement of a claim (that is distinct from the claim to compensation). Since a harm is merely a setback to an interest, there are ways of setting back a person's interest without infringing on a claim. For example, if Al wins over the heart of Bob's fiancée, Al harms Bob without owing him compensation. It is not clear that enslaving a person and releasing him right before reproduction violates a duty to his progeny. Such a violation presupposes that a person has a claim that others not harm her parents before she comes into existence.[19] This involves a rather expansive view of persons' claims on others. If such expansive claims exist, and I doubt they do, then the acts maintaining slavery for the last generation of slaves may well generate a claim to compensation in at least some of their descendants.

Conclusion

Slavery itself probably has not resulted in a compensable injury to the descendants of slaves. If the descendants have a legitimate claim to compensation, then there must be other grounds for the claim.

PART 3
Compensation May Be Owed to the Descendants of Slaves As a Result of a Legitimate Inheritance Claim

Compensation As the Justified Removal of Unjust Benefits

A descendant of slaves may not exist in the relevant possible world, hence, cannot legitimately claim to have been harmed in the actual world. Still, in the actual world, white males have benefited from past injustices by gaining unwarranted self-esteem[20] or an unfair competitive advantage, and it may be argued that compensatory justice requires that these benefits be returned.

The problem with this compensatory account is that even if white males have benefited from these past unjust acts, compensatory justice does not require that the unjust gains be transferred from them to uninjured parties. Such a move would at most transfer the injustice in the distribution of unjust benefits rather than eliminating this benefit. For example, imagine that Alice steals Betty's Mercedes Benz, sells the car, and uses the money to finance an expensive medical-school education for her daughter, Carol, where Carol does not know of the source of this money. Carol has a medical school degree that is, at least in part, the result of an unjust act. However, if the value of this degree, or any part of it, is transferred to an innocent third party, this does not eliminate the injustice but merely transfers it, and compensatory justice does not require this sort of transfer. In affirmative action, for example, if some of the unjust benefits of slavery are transferred from white males to racial minorities who have not been injured (at least not from slavery), this merely transfers the unjust benefits from one innocent person to another.

Models of Compensation

One might argue that the slaves are owed compensation, but since they have died, their moral claims are transferred to their inheritors, usually their descendants, through implicit inheritance practices or through a will.[21] I am assuming here that the right of the original property owner to give away her property and the right of the inheritor to receive the property are essential elements of property rights, and that property rights entail prima facie moral duties. According to this account, if the enslaved person had not been enslaved in the relevantly similar possible world, and if the slave's inheritors are the rightful owners of the slave's property and if the inheritors of the slave's property are likely her descendants, then compensatory justice supports compensation being owed to the slave's descendants. Note that this account does not rest on the claim that the current descendants of slaves were harmed by slavery, thus it escapes concerns that relate to their nonexistence in the relevant possible world.

A different but related account is that the slave retains her moral claim to compensation even after her death and this claim survives her death. On this account, the descendants never own the claim to compensation but merely assert it on behalf of the deceased slaves in the same way in which an estate's trustee may claim (both morally and legally) the right to recover money owed to the deceased after she dies. On this account, the descendants have a second-order right to assert the first-order rights of the deceased slaves, and the compensation is owed to the slaves themselves. And, given that the trustees of the slaves' estates are probably their descendants, the descendants may choose to distribute the money to themselves.

This second model does not have an inheritance element, since current blacks never have a right against the party that owes compensation. My assumption here is that, in general, a third-party beneficiary does not have a (first-order) right against the person against whom the right is held. I do allow that the descendants have a second-order right against whoever owes a debt of compensation to the slaves. The second-order right here is analogous to the way in which a corporate officer has the legal standing to demand the satisfaction of the corporation's claim without himself being the claim holder. Perhaps the officer does not have a right so much as a narrow, contract-based power. By analogy, the descendant has the (moral) power to demand the satisfaction of the debt that is owed to the slave.

The point has been raised whether the better analogy is that the descendants are the trustees, the beneficiaries, or the beneficiaries of a constructive trust.[22] A constructive trust is not a trust but a legal remedy imposed by a court in cases involving unjust enrichment and either fraud or unconscionable conduct.[23] It need not reflect the intent of the property owner. Examples of cases in which it is used include where a beneficiary kills the testator, or where he suppresses a later will. In contrast, a trust is an intended arrangement where a trustee manages, invests, or safeguards the trust assets for the benefit of certain beneficiaries. Both are legal entities. The moral analogue here is the arrangement where the slave retains rights to the property (i.e., the claim to compensation), but the descendant is either the administrator or the intended beneficiary. In some cases, the intended beneficiary is picked out via the slave's counterfactual intent, since in many cases the slave did not recognize that she is owed compensation and thus did not form an intent or a desire as to how it ought to be distributed upon her death. Since the slave's counterfactual intent would likely have been that his descendants fill both roles, I think that both models are useful for getting at the moral analogue.

The idea that a person may have a moral claim or an interest in receiving just compensation even after her death can be seen in Joel Feinberg's account of postmortem harms.[24] Feinberg argues that a person's interest may survive her death even though she does not survive her death. Feinberg's idea is that the person's particular goals and desires can be satisfied or frustrated by events that she is not aware of and that occur after her death. For example, Ms. Cohen's desire that her son, Eric, become a rabbi may be satisfied by her son's achievement even after Ms. Cohen dies (and thus ceases to exist). On Feinberg's account since a person's interests can be satisfied by events or states of affairs that occur after her death, that person's interests survive her death. Feinberg asserts that while a subsequent event may *make it true* that a surviving interest is set back, the event does not *cause* the interest to be set back. Since, on his account, the makes-it-true relation is not indexed to a particular time, postmortem events may satisfy or set back (i.e., harm) a person's interests. For example, Eric's graduation from rabbinical school makes it true that his mother's desire is satisfied, hence makes it true that during his mother's lifetime, a significant desire of hers is satisfied.

In the case of the descendants, if failure to pay compensation to the slave sets back the slave's interest in being treated in a just manner, the postmortem failure may be an unjust omission that grounds a legitimate claim to compensation.

Note that neither this account nor the earlier inheritance account assumes that the descendants must exist in the relevantly similar possible world in order to have a legitimate claim to compensation. And the second account does not even assume that the descendants of slaves have a significant claim to compensation, since on this account any failure to pay compensation is wrongful primarily because it sets back the first-order rights or interests of the slaves. These objections thus avoid the problem of the nonexistence of the descendants of slavery in the relevantly similar possible world without slavery, while at the same time they provide a reason to think that compensatory justice supports compensatory programs such as affirmative action and the payment of reparations. This is not to say that such compensatory programs are all-things-considered morally justified, for they may still be overridden by conflicting moral reasons.

The Argument for the Inheritance Model

The inheritance model is a better model than the one in which the slave retains her right to compensation and her descendants act as the trustees of her claim. This is because giving money to the descendants would often not satisfy the slave's right. The idea behind the trustee model is that the slave has a right to compensation, and that it should be given to the person or persons to whom the slave wanted the compensation to go, or at least would have wanted it to go had she thought about it. It seems likely, however, that in a significant number of cases the slave would have preferred that the compensation be given to groups other than descendants several generations removed. For example, she may have preferred that it be given to her close friends, African relatives, or the Baptist church.

A proponent of the trustee model may respond that the slave probably did desire (or would have desired had she considered it) that the compensation be given to her children or grandchildren. The proponent might then reason that the slave's children or grandchildren probably did desire (or would have desired had they thought about it) that the money be given to their children or grandchildren, and so on. On such a model, the trusteeship would end up with the descendants of slaves getting the money via interlocking desires. The problem with this solution is that the slave probably would have desired (or would have desired) not just that her wealth go to certain persons but that her claim be transferred as well. Given this desire, it is not clear why one would hold that the slave's right is retained by her rather than transferred to her descendants via interlocking desires.

One might object that the inheritance model mistakenly assumes that inheritance of claims can exist in a moral sense that is independent of the conventions that characterize legal inheritance. There is a view of inheritance that does allow it to be conceptually preinstitutional. If inheritance is, in principle, merely a gift (or a contract), and if gifts (or contracts) are a type of promise, and if promises are preinstitutional practices that create moral duties in the promisor, then inheritance is preinstitutional.[25] On this account, a claim of inheritance is nothing more than a claim to be given the object of a promise. Now this may differ from the legal institution of inheritance that includes both mandatory and default rules with regard to the disposition of a person's property. Such rules may be justified by other concerns (e.g., fairness, utility, concern for the welfare of the deceased's spouse and children), but they are not essential features of inheritance. If this is correct, then the inheritance model is consistent with preinstitutional rights, hence, independent of legal conventions or institutions.

Groups Are Not Owed Compensation

Some proponents of reparations argue that blacks *qua group* have a legitimate claim to compensation.[26] If a group is understood as something other than a collection of individuals (or in some cases a collection of individuals standing in certain relations to one another), then such a claim is problematic.[27] This is because an entity can have a legitimate claim of justice only if it has the capacity to enjoy different levels of well-being (i.e., a life that can go better or worse). This can be seen in that all three types of justice (i.e., retributive, compensatory, and distributive) are concerned with levels of well-being. An entity can enjoy different levels of well-being only if it has desires, and a being can have desires only if it is conscious.[28] It is hard to imagine an entity that cannot be healthy or ill, comfortable or uncomfortable, happy or unhappy, satisfied or unsatisfied, or successful or frustrated with regard to a project, having its life go better or worse. Plants, for example, may thrive or not thrive, but it is hard to see how their lives might go better or worse. Hence, *qua group* blacks do not have a legitimate claim to compensation, although *qua collection* blacks or the descendants of slaves may have a claim to compensation.

The Amount of Inheritance

According to the inheritance model, descendants are owed the compensation owed to their enslaved ancestors. Compensation for slavery should attempt to place a slave in the position that she would have been in but for slavery. If a person is enslaved, some damages may be required for quality of life lost when the person was forcibly removed from Africa. This may include lost access to the slave's family, friends, and culture. If the slave is then forced to work in the United States, this also calls for compensation.[29] That a slave would have died but for the institution of slavery does not undermine her claim to compensation. For example, consider the case where pain and suffering worth $500,000 is imposed on a slave who is raped by her master, where had she not been enslaved, she would have been gang raped (far more frequently) and slaughtered by an aggressor rival tribe in Africa. Determining which possible world is the baseline for comparison is a complex task. It sometimes involves selecting a possible world without a number of unjust acts rather than the one without only the injustice done by the person whose debt of compensation we are trying to measure. This can be seen in the above rape case.

Other things being equal, the amount of compensation owed to an injured person as a matter of justice is that amount of wealth required to place her at the point of indifference. This is the point at which she is indifferent between being injured and compensated and being uninjured.[30] One method for determining the amount of damages for slavery is to imagine the *ex ante* transaction where a potential slave is asked to determine the minimum price for her to accept a particular chance (e.g., n percent, of being enslaved). The compensation owed is then set equal to the amount divided by n percent. For example, if a person were to accept a 10 percent chance of being enslaved for $1 million, then the amount of damages owed would be $10 million. This model has the advantage of allowing the slave herself to determine the disvalue of slavery. It also gives us a practical guide, since we can look at the actual premium workers that charge on dangerous professions as a crude guide to this amount.[31] In specifying this counterfactual, we would have to fix the person's context (e.g., her level of wealth, expectations, risk aversion, and country of residence), a task that lies outside the scope of this chapter.[32] The standard is a function of the slave's individual preferences, although for practical reasons statistical generalizations may have to be relied upon. A second method involves an estimation of the slave's lost income based on the market value of a free worker performing the labor done by the slave. This method measures the actual wages lost by a particular slave and could be used along with the first method.

PART 4
Conclusion

The claim of descendants of slaves to compensation for slavery is dependent upon their owning the slave's claim to compensation via inheritance. Insofar as this right has been infringed upon, they have suffered a token harm. This token harm does not depend on their having been harmed by slavery or on the slaves retaining their rights to compensation. The token harm of lost inheritance, and this harm alone, grounds their claim to compensation for slavery. This compensation is owed to individuals, not to a group, and it is equal to the amount of resources required to place them at the point of indifference.

5

Reject the Inheritance-Based Claim to Reparations

In the previous chapter, I argued that the claim of descendants of slaves to compensation for slavery depends on their owning the slave's claim to compensation via inheritance. The relevant harm consists of lost inheritance, and this harm alone grounds their claim to compensation for slavery. This compensation is equal to the amount of resources required to place them at the point of indifference. In this chapter, I argue that there are fatal problems with the inheritance-based claim.

PART 1
Objections to the Inheritance-Based Claim to Reparations

THE METAPHYSICAL OBJECTION: THE CLAIM DIVIDES OVER SUCCESSIVE GENERATIONS

On the above account, the inherited claim is divided among increasingly large numbers of descendants as successive generations come about. As a person's descendants branch out over successive generations, each generation gains only a portion of the earlier generation's claim. For example, if a black man is owed $1,000,000 in compensation and his claim is divided up equally between ten great grandchildren, each will have a claim worth no more than $100,000 plus interest. Of course, the interest owed may be substantial, given the length of time over which the claim has persisted.

The Epistemic Objection: Problems in Assessing the Amount Owed

Over several generations, epistemic problems arise in identifying the descendants of slaves as the inheritors of the slave's claim. The notion that a claim would have been passed on through successive generations is made less likely by the proliferation of factors that lead families, over generations, to lose wealth, to sell off claims in return for immediate benefits, or to disinherit one another. These factors make it unlikely that later descendants would have a portion of the share, let alone the whole share, of their ancestors' claim. Even the notion that as a collection current black descendants of slaves would hold the claims to compensation of the slaves also depends on a denial of transference between the group of descendants and others that is improbable.

An additional epistemic problem arises with regard to the amount of the original claim. Other than by a counterfactual free market in which persons sell themselves into slavery, it seems hard to assign a value to the loss of liberty, pain and suffering, degradation, etc. The slave's (and her family's) *ex ante* wealth and expectations about quality of life in Africa would play a large role in determining the counterfactual contract price. In assigning the disvalue of slavery, a potential slave would compare the disvalue of a life in slavery to the value of resources being provided to her family and village. The idea behind the resources being provided to the slave's family and village rather than the slave herself relates to the notion that a slave, being the property of another (the master), would not be able to retain the resources. That is, any resources given to a slave can, and probably will, be confiscated by her master, thus making such payments of dubious value. If instead the slave can redirect the benefits to someone who is unowned, then in some sense she can get something of value in return for her enslavement.

The epistemic problem cannot be solved via an assumption that but for slavery or past discrimination blacks would have the same income and distribution of positions as whites. This is because there is strong evidence to believe that there are genetic differences in the average intelligence of racial groups and that such differences will likely affect a group's economic performance.[1] Also, there are probably differences in sociocultural beliefs, attitudes, and values between different groups.[2] While not genetic, these are deeply embedded factors that are also likely to affect a group's economic performance. In addition, there are destructive behaviors that are not the result of discrimination and that likely produce inequality between racial groups. Consider, for example, the high out-of-wedlock birthrate and disproportionately large amount of violent crimes in the black community. These are, in general, voluntary acts for which moral responsibility rests on the agent who performs them. When such acts form a general pattern in the black community, they produce an unequal distribution of income and wealth when compared to other racial groups. The effects of this destructive behavior must be disentangled from those injuries that result from the loss of inheritance, and this is a very difficult task. When combined, these epistemic problems make the decision as to the amount of damages owed for lost inheritance highly speculative.

One objection likely to arise here is that the differences in intelligence, sociocultural beliefs and values, crime rates, etc. between the descendants of slaves and other U.S. populations are the effects of slavery and related oppression (e.g., segregation and widespread racism).[3] This claim is not obvious. For example, interracial adoption studies provide evidence that there is a genetic explanation of interracial differences in intelligence.[4] If intelligence affects such things as poverty, schooling, welfare dependency, parenting, and crime, then there is a nondiscriminatory explanation of some of the interracial differences in these areas.[5] However, even if these genetic explanations fail, we think that many persons, even ones from rotten social backgrounds, are morally responsible for a good deal of their acts, despite the etiology of these actions. If this is correct, then it further seems that a person may not collect for harmful or self-destructive behavior for which he is fully responsible. To see this, consider where a man gets his car dented due to another driver's negligence. As a result of his anger over the accident, he gives his wife a severe beating, thereby grounding a just claim in her to compensation. It intuitively seems that the negligent driver may not be made to pay the husband's debt to his wife, despite the driver's having caused her injury. I leave aside what accounts for this result (e.g., intervention by a morally responsible agent, the unforeseeability of this result, the limited scope of the driver's duty, or the lack of proximate causation). If we assume that justice presupposes that the victim and wrongdoer are morally responsible parties, and I think we should, then any blanket denial of responsibility would undercut the descendants' claim of compensatory justice.

The slaveholders are long dead, and the wealth of the taxpayer population has been formed in large part through voluntary actions, thus creating a powerful moral claim against overcompensation of the descendants. This claim rests on the value of respecting reasonable expectations, protecting legitimate property rights, promoting economic efficiency, and perhaps also satisfying economic desert. An extended defense of this claim will take us too far afield, but I note that many justifications of property rights and free-market transactions are independent of claims about the justice of the initial acquisition of resources.[6] Given this powerful claim on behalf of taxpayers, and given the speculative nature of the descendants' claim, the case for compensation should be rejected.

In addition, merely having benefited from a wrongdoing is not enough to establish liability. To see this, consider the Jim and Frank case (the two tennis players, where the better player, Frank, is stabbed, and as a result Jim wins more tournaments and money), discussed in chapter 2. There our intuitions were that Jim does not owe his increased winnings to Frank, despite the fact that but for the injustice Frank would have won the money. Whether this result is explained by Jim's income being at least in part the result of desert, legitimate property rights in the tournament's owners, or the role of merit is an issue that need not be resolved here.

Nor can the epistemic problems be solved via a setting of compensation equal to the disgorgement of ill-gotten gains. This is because disgorgement is not directly related to the attempt to return the descendants to the position that they would have been in but for the harmful act or omission.[7] In general, a person who injures another may have an unjust gain that differs from the victim's unjust loss. Consider the following case: Jane has $10,000 in the bank and has it invested at a 6 percent rate of interest. Susan then steals the money and invests it in a risky technology company whose stock subsequently skyrockets, resulting in Susan's stock (at least that part purchased with Jane's money) being worth $200,000. Here Susan's unjust gain is far greater than the sum needed to compensate Jane for her loss.[8]

The Offset Objections: Violent Crime and Welfare Benefits

Blacks commit a substantial number of crimes, including a disproportionately large number of violent crimes. For example, approximately one black male in four is incarcerated at some time for the commission of a felony (note that this figure includes both violent and nonviolent crimes).[9] Given that crimes that victimize others ground a claim to compensation in the victim, the compensation for lost inheritance must be offset by such claims to compensation against those who have committed such acts, or those who have benefited from the inability or refusal of aggressors to pay compensation. To the extent that this affects a substantial portion of the black community (e.g., some criminals and their families), this may reduce the compensation that is owed. Whether this offset exceeds the compensation owed introduces yet another epistemic difficulty, and the problem gets even murkier when we consider the party against whom the offset applies.

One other offset that is mentioned in the literature and that is worth considering is that accompanying the welfare state. Michael Levin argues that in the United States, there is an enormous transfer of wealth from whites to blacks every year. He argues that since blacks make considerably less money, on average, than do whites, since blacks constitute about 40 percent of welfare dependency, and since income taxes are progressive, there is a net annual white-to-black transfer of about $75 billion.[10] Using 1990 dollars, this is equivalent to a Marshall Plan for blacks every three years. Such payments probably do not count toward any reparations owed, since the money is given out in a manner that is unrelated to reparations and is instead based on need.

Consider the case where a wealthy benefactor, Al, negligently breaks the leg of his grandson, Stan. Before he can pay for that injury, Al dies, and his estate, using its discretion, decides to transfer to each of his three grandsons, including Stan, $300,000. Does this satisfy the debt? If the estate labels the money to Stan "payment plus a gift," then it does (assuming that this amount is more than the debt), whereas if it does not do so, then the case gets murkier. The problem here is that there is an issue as to whether transfers of wealth that are not intended to satisfy a debt of compensation, not labeled as such, and not accompanied by a relevant type of illocutionary act can satisfy a debt of compensation. It seems that this is likely not the case where the money is given to the injured party in satisfaction of an independent moral claim (e.g., the moral claim that all of those in need receive equal treatment). Hence, this white-to-black transfer will probably not satisfy even a portion of the debt owed for slavery.

Conclusion

The division of the claim lessens a descendant's claim to compensation. The offset difficulties challenge the notion that, on average, any sum is owed to the descendants of slaves. This is because many of the persons who claim compensation on the basis of lost inheritance may end up owing more money to fellow citizens than they are owed. The epistemic difficulties cloud the case for reparations, since they highlight the fact that the claim to reparations must compete against the claim to whatever grounds the private ownership of property, and that the relative strength of the reparations claim depends on the accurate assessment of the amount of lost inheritance. Since the accurate assessment is unlikely, the case for reparations weakens considerably.

PART 2
Who Owes Compensation?

The persons who captured, traded, and owned slaves as part of the American slave trade are no longer alive and do not have current estates. If compensation is owed, the issue arises as to the entity that ought to pay it. The proponents of compensation often propose that the federal government pay out the compensation. Other entities that might be asked to pay compensation are state governments and the beneficiaries of the persons who captured, traded, and owned slaves.

The Federal Government

The Federal Government's Role in Permitting Slavery

In general, the federal government permitted but did not cause enslavement and the slave trade to occur. Generally, a party does not owe compensation for harm to another for a refusal to act, unless the refusal infringed upon a special duty that was owed to the harmed party. This special duty might rest on either a contract or a special relationship. However, neither is present in this case. There was no contract between the potential slaves and the federal government, nor did the institution of slavery violate the terms of the prewar Constitution. This is because the Constitution explicitly recognized slavery (e.g., Art. I, Sec. 2). In addition, the federal government's role was explicitly limited (by Art. I, Sec. 8) to certain enumerated functions. These do not include preventing injustices committed by the states or private individuals. One might argue that the federal government had a special relationship to all of its citizens based on whatever justification warrants the federal government's authority, and that this special relationship gave rise to the duty in question. This does not follow, however, since the government's authority is limited to a specific list of enumerated powers, and this structure precludes action designed to satisfy the alleged duty.

To the extent that the federal government did cause or actively maintain slavery, this argument ought to be rejected. An example of where the federal government may have maintained slavery was via its enforcement of the fugitive slave laws.[11] However, to the extent that the federal government merely permitted the laws to be enforced by state or private agents, and to the extent that state governments nullified them, the federal government's causal role is lessened. Among the states that nullified these laws were Massachusetts and Vermont in 1843, Illinois in 1853, and Wisconsin in 1854. Also, the federal government would then owe compensation only to those slaves and their descendants for whom the enforcement of these laws kept them in slavery, whether this occurred by force, deterrence, or incapacitation, or by a contribution to the viability of the slave trade. Thus whether the fugitive slave laws involved the government causing or maintaining slaves depends on the empirical issue of whether its agents (e.g., federal marshals) actively recaptured or helped recapture escaped slaves.

National Identity

George Schedler argues against reparations based on the notion that the prewar federal government is not strictly identical to the postwar federal government. His argument for this rests on a change in the fundamental assumption of racial inequality that can be seen in the passage of the Thirteenth, Fourteenth, and Fifteenth Amendments.[12] This argument is, at the least, incomplete and probably incorrect. A legal system can change some of its more fundamental laws as long as it does so in a way that satisfies the rule of recognition (the litmus for what shall constitute a law in a particular system of law). If this were not the case, then it would be a contradiction to say that a nation has changed some of its fundamental laws, and it is not. Schedler might argue that the postwar legal changes did not satisfy the rule of recognition because of the process in which the Southern states were coerced into ratifying these amendments. However, at the very least, such an argument would have to be made and would require the further argument that a particular system of law is an essential property of a nation.

Schedler's argument is also irrelevant. Consider this analogy. If Sony buys Toyota, then in the absence of a contractual condition to the contrary, Sony assumes all of Toyota's debts and assets. If the postwar federal government legitimately replaced the antebellum government, then in the absence of a contractual condition to the contrary the postwar government assumed all of the prewar government's debts and assets. In the case of the alleged two governments, there is no such contractual condition, hence, the postwar government would still hold such debts.

On a side note, if one thinks, and this is obviously controversial, that the Civil War was an illegal war of aggression, then the federal government's debt to blacks might have to compete with its debt to Civil War-era Southerners and their descendants.[13] This would introduce a need for a theory of debt prioritization.

State Governments and the Beneficiaries of the Slave Trade

The case for state governments being required to pay compensation is stronger than that of the federal government, since the former are not contractually prevented from protecting the basic rights of their citizens, and since the states played a more active role in maintaining slavery than the federal government. Also, it might be argued that enough U.S. citizens have benefited from slavery to require as an administrative matter that the citizenry pay compensation. However, the above epistemic, metaphysical, and offset problems still weigh against requiring payment from the state or the citizenry.

In addition, the case for requiring payment from the beneficiaries of slavery is even weaker, since having benefited from an unjust practice does not by itself establish a duty to compensate the victim. As a matter of compensatory justice, a person owes compensation for a harmful injustice only if he was causally involved in the injustice or his token benefit is the same as the victim's token harm (e.g., he received a stolen good). The idea behind this account is that compensatory justice is concerned with the rectification of rights-infringing harm.[14] Where a person harmed another, even in the absence of fault, such rectification is, as a matter of justice, required of the agent that brought about the harm. Also, where a person innocently receives a stolen good, the person lacks the procedural pedigree required for legitimate ownership of it, and it ought to be returned to the person who has it.[15] However, where a person merely benefits from an injustice, as in the case of the tennis professionals, Jim and Frank, the benefit may have proper procedural pedigree. If this is correct, then current U.S. citizens do not owe compensation to the descendants of slaves if a substantial portion of them did not receive a particular good that was stolen or defrauded from a victim, and this is likely the case.

It might be objected that most wealth in the United States is tainted by past injustice. The idea here is that if a tangible good was acquired via an injustice, then its pedigree prevents legitimate ownership unless it is returned to the victim of the injustice or her inheritor.[16] This is analogous to the way in which a false premise in an otherwise sound argument undermines the conclusion. However, this objection proves too much, since given the sea of injustices that has characterized human history, this threatens to undermine almost all current ownership. To the extent that one adopts a procedural account of current private property rights, there has to be a time frame that limits the scope of injustices that will undermine the legitimacy of particular holdings. I leave aside the issue of whether this limitation is metaphysical or merely epistemic.

This objection weakens where the property has changed form over successive generations. Consider a case in which a person stole a cow in the 1850s and used it to buy supplies to start a business that he gave to his children, who then sold it to pay for the medical education of their children. In such a case, there is no concrete entity that is passed down and the gains are mixed with the labor of the different persons. The epistemic difficulties in assessing the value taken and the contribution of different persons probably make this objection succeed only at the cost of undermining the dominant nonconsequentialist justifications of private property and thus of compensatory justice. This is because there is a close link between compensatory justice and a system of private property rights. In particular, it is hard to see how a system of individual nonpunitive liability could occur in a system in which persons are not assigned control over particular resources. Perhaps the two could occur together in a system justified via forward-looking reasons.[17] If, however, such a justification does not succeed, and I suggest but do not defend the claim that it will not, then the objection undermines itself by undercutting a requirement of compensatory justice.

PART 3
Conclusion

Slavery harmed the slaves but not their descendants, since slavery brought about their existence. The descendants gain the slaves' claims via inheritance. However, collecting the inheritance-based claim runs into a number of difficulties. First, every descendant usually has no more than a portion of the slave's claim, because the claim is often divided over generations. Second, there are epistemic difficulties involving the ownership of the claim, since it is unlikely that a descendant of a slave several generations removed would have retained the claim of inheritance given the loss of wealth and disinheritance that often characterizes families. There are also problems in determining the amount of inheritance. This is in part because of the problems of calculating in the effects of offsets, especially crime-related offsets, which are owed by a significant portion of the descendants. Even if this inheritance claim can be established with sufficient confidence, certain entities may not be asked to pay it. The federal government does not owe compensation, since as a historical matter it permitted but did not cause enslavement. The beneficiaries of slavery do not owe compensation, since merely receiving the benefit of an unjust activity does not by itself generate a debt of compensation. When combined, these problems constitute an overwhelming case against reparations.

SECTION 5

Proper Respect

6

Intrinsic Moral Value and Racial Differences

PART 1
The Expression of Equal Moral Value

RESPECT FOR PERSONS AND EXPRESSION

In the last four chapters we have seen that where the state fails to implement strong affirmative-action programs or provide reparations for slavery, this does not infringe on current black persons' right to compensation. In chapter 1, it was argued that state refusal to prevent workplace discrimination probably also is not a right infringement. Still, one might wonder whether the state's refusal to provide compensation constitutes a failure to condemn past injustices and thereby results in the state failing to express blacks' equal moral worth.

The idea here is the Kantian notion that at its core, justice focuses on whether our thoughts and actions express persons' equal moral value. The idea here is that the Kantian imperative prohibits certain ways of thinking and acting toward persons (i.e., in degrading, unequal, and nonuniversalizable ways). These ways are not solely a function of persons' specific rights (e.g., rights to property). The prohibited type of disrespect might be viewed as a type of right violation if persons have perfect duties not to express contempt for other people. The value of such expression is understood in terms of its fittingness rather than its role in communication.[1] For example, consider where a criminal rapes and kills a mother. The duty to respect the woman and the killer requires that her family condemn him.[2] Similarly, after the Holocaust, the nation-states were obligated to condemn the behavior of the Nazi elites. Some expressivist theories assert that such a duty justifies punishment, since it can account for both our intuitions on proportionality and the constraint against torture.[3] Such a duty also is argued to establish the wrongfulness of the United States allowing immigrants to come to this country in return for their waiving all rights to non-emergency welfare benefits, even where such a trade neither infringes on the immigrants' specific rights nor is exploitative.[4] On this account, the state might express contempt for black persons by failing to compensate them for past injustices. Such a failure may express the notion that past injustices can be ignored since blacks have less moral value than other persons.

On this account, an act that is neither exploitative nor rights-infringing can express contempt for a person and thereby fail to respect her as a person. In general, a behavior is expressive of an attitude or a proposition just in case it exhibits that attitude or puts forth a proposition. This is probably a function of the agent's motive, intent, or the social understanding of her act. For example, one disrespectful act may involve the agent being motivated by the view that the person toward whom she acts has less intrinsic value than other persons, she intends to convey that view, and that is how her act is generally understood. On some accounts, this expression is independent of whether the attitude or proposition is actually conveyed to an audience on a particular occasion, and on some accounts on all occasions. In the case of black persons, the contempt likely involves the notion that they have less intrinsic value than do other persons. Treatment that expresses the notion that blacks have less than equal value does not disrespect them as persons if they have, on average, less intrinsic value than other persons. In this chapter, I consider whether this is the case.

The background notion here is that there are only three ways in which a person through his action can disrespect another. The three can be seen in the two types of disrespect that might occur. The first type of disrespect is a function of the way in which the disrespected person is treated. This is the type of disrespect seen from the perspective of a person who is the object of an action (i.e., object-centered disrespect). On this account, a person's rights form the perimeter defining the realm of permissible interference in his life. Where an agent passes this perimeter, the invasion prevents, or at least reduces, the autonomous right holder's opportunity to shape his own life. The second type of disrespect is a function of the attitude that the agent through his action expresses toward the disrespected person. This is the type of disrespect from the perspective of the agent who exhibits the disrespect (i.e., subject-centered disrespect). Here the agent through his action expresses the proposition that the targeted person has no, or an inappropriately small amount of, intrinsic value. One common way this is done is where the agent takes advantage of a weaker person's desperation to form a contract in which the stronger person treats the weaker one as a mere tool by which to gain an unfair amount of the transactional benefit. Here the weaker person gives his valid consent, but the stronger person's attitude toward him is still objectionable. The three ways of disrespect are designed to track the two types of disrespect, object- and subject-centered disrespect, with the disrespect manifested in exploitation illustrating a particularly common form of agent-centered disrespect. This three-part test is general and not confined to hiring or admission to a university.

The Message of Affirmative Action

An important example of this argument is one by Thomas E. Hill Jr., who argues that a central purpose of affirmative action should be to communicate a message.[5] That message in the context of university admission and hiring is the following: the university community (or the state) asks for the trust of minorities and women. As evidence of the state's or community's sincerity, it offers minorities and women full membership in the university community. This offer involves the creation of special opportunities by which the community (or state) recognizes the disadvantages that these persons have suffered and at the same time shows respect for their talents and commitment to the university's ideals.[6] On Hill's account, the value of this message is not just a means to a future good or a dutiful payment of debt but rather a way of bringing about a certain type of relation between persons over time (including both the past and future). This relation is a historical and biographical one that embodies a commitment to fair opportunity and mutual respect. Hill's theory is important because it directly relates the issue of affirmative action to the criterion for respect for persons.

It is controversial whether this theory correctly identifies a criterion of respect for persons. This can be seen if we focus on two theories of expressive action. On an externalist account, an act expresses a message through conventional symbols. If the message of affirmative action or reparations (or the refusal to implement them) is understood in these terms, then the theory provides a forward-looking justification of such programs in terms of the communication of various ideas rather than a justice-based justification of them.

On an internalist account, the connection between the act and the message it expresses is internal to the act. One immediate problem here is to fill out this internal connection. For example, it is unclear whether it is conceptual or metaphysical. On this second account, the message is likely identified with the agent's intent or motive rather than the message that the audience receives and the means by which it is expressed. Since the concern over respect for persons is an inquiry into the right, this theory results in the right being a function of the agent's motive. This introduces a second problem, which is that motive probably does not affect the rightness of an act.[7]

Despite these problems, the expressivist theory has a couple of advantageous features. First, it connects the issue of affirmative action to the fundamental issue in deontological ethics. Second, it provides a test for the moral status of affirmative action, which is whether it expresses the equal value of persons in general and of racial groups in particular. This test thus links deontology to the notion that persons are fundamentally equal.

Thesis

I argue below for the following thesis: racial and ethnic groups differ in their per capita intrinsic moral value. This is relevant to the expressive content of the refusal to implement affirmative-action and reparations programs, insofar as these are interpreted as expressing the notion that such groups are not of equal value. My argument rests on the notion that autonomy is a ground for intrinsic moral value, and the notion that there are individual and group differences in autonomy. I then argue that the implications of this per capita difference between racial and ethnic groups are in some cases significant in that they are relevant to both public policy and private action.

PART 2
The Argument

My argument for the thesis is as follows:

(P1) Other things equal, intrinsic moral value is proportional to autonomy.
(P2) Other things equal, autonomy is proportional to intelligence.
(C1) Hence, other things equal, intrinsic moral value is proportional to intelligence. [(P1), (P2)]
(P3) Whites and Asians have greater per capita levels of intelligence than blacks.
(C2) Hence, other things equal, whites and Asians have greater per capita intrinsic moral value than blacks. [(C1), (P3)]
(P4) Other factors do not offset this difference in per capita moral value.
(C3) Hence, all things considered, whites and Asians have greater per capita intrinsic moral value than blacks. [(C2), (P4)]

A thing is intrinsically valuable if it is valuable in and of itself, that is, its value is independent of any relation to something else. Intrinsic value may be further capable of being filled out in terms of the notions of intrinsic goodness and intrinsic badness, where these are then viewed as primitive notions.

I use the phrase "intrinsic moral value" to distinguish the type of value concerning morality from other types of intrinsic value, for example, prudential and aesthetic. This, however, does not entail that all of the grounds of intrinsic moral value are conceptually dependent on moral notions. Some grounds (e.g., pleasure) are not.

Intrinsic value is a property of states of affairs and perhaps also other types of entities (e.g., persons). Insofar as nonconsequentialism is true, that is, the obligatory action is not necessarily that action that brings about the state of affairs with the greatest intrinsic moral value, the value of a person (or the state of affairs involving her existence) is not immediately related to how she may be treated. As a result, I keep separate my analyses with regard to each of these properties.

All of the above premises is controversial and requires a defense. I shall defend them in order.

Intrinsic Moral Value Is in Part a Function of Intelligence

(P1) puts forth the notion that autonomy is a ground of intrinsic moral value, and (P2) puts forth the notion that the amount of autonomy that a being has is in part a function of its intelligence.

Autonomy Is a Ground of Intrinsic Moral Value

Autonomy is the capacity to evaluate and choose among competing desires and beliefs and to effectuate these choices. The model of autonomy that I adopt involves a variant on Harry Frankfurt's theory of a person and freedom of the will.[8] On his account, a person has first-order desires, which are desires to do or not do a particular action, and second-order desires, which are desires to have or not have a particular first-order desire.[9] A parallel structure holds with regard to beliefs. On my variant of his theory, an agent is morally responsible for her actions only if she has the capacity to form second-order desires (and beliefs) that determine which first-order desires (and beliefs) bring about her actions. Frankfurt calls these effective second-order desires "second-order volitions." The basic idea of my variant on Frankfurt's theory is that autonomy involves two elements. First, it involves the capacity of an agent to choose on the basis of higher-order desires (and higher-order beliefs) with which she identifies which desires (and beliefs) guide her actions (and thoughts). Second, it involves the capacity of the agent to effectuate the chosen first-order desires (and first-order beliefs) into action (and thought). This theory of autonomy is a variant on Frankfurt's, because his theory does not clearly provide room for beliefs and is not a theory of autonomy. For the purposes of simplicity, I will leave out the discussion of beliefs in the following discussion of autonomy.

The capacity of an agent to choose on the basis of higher-order desires with which she identifies which desires guide her actions, allows an agent to constitute herself through the process of adopting and rejecting desires. There is thus a close link between a person's actions and her identity. On my theory, it is in part the capacity to control her actions through her higher-order desires that makes a moral agent responsible for her actions. If we define "person" as "a being with second-order volitions and second-order beliefs," then there is a close relation between autonomy and personhood, with the latter property being included in the former.

The capacities that underlie autonomy are also some of, if not all of, the capacities that make a person morally responsible for her behavior and the more a person has these capacities, the more responsible she is for her acts, other things being equal. It does not follow from this, however, that a person with more autonomy will, on average, satisfy her moral duties more often and to a greater degree than someone with less autonomy.[10] Hence, it is possible that a person with great autonomy uses these capacities while acting wrongly.

The notion that an autonomous person must not only be able to evaluate first-order desires but must also be able to put them into effect can be seen via thought experiments where persons lack this capacity. So, for example, if a person has the capacity to evaluate her first-order desires but cannot effectuate them because of paralysis or an inadequate range of options, we would not say of her that she is autonomous. For example, imagine a person who is trapped in a very tight pit that allows her no limb movement. She can merely eat and drink the food and water that periodically falls into it. She also has no contact with sentient beings. We would not say of her that she is autonomous. Similarly, imagine a person who is unable to think or do anything other than escape a fierce carnivorous animal that constantly hunts her, where escaping it requires every mental and physical resource she has.[11] Intuitively, this person is not autonomous.

The higher-order desires probably do not stand merely in a one-directional linear relation to the first-order desires. Rather, the first-order desires must cohere with the higher-order desires (and perhaps also many of the other first-order desires). This coherence relation is analogous to that posited by coherentist theories of epistemic justification.[12] There are several advantages to this coherentist account of this feature of autonomy. First, such an account can avoid the problem of an infinite regress of desires. In particular, it need not posit an infinite regress of successively higher-order desires, each of which evaluates the immediately lower-level desires. Nor need it posit an arbitrary level at which higher-order desires are no longer evaluated. Second, it can provide a powerful account of self-governance, a notion that lies at the heart of autonomy. On this theory, a person is self-governed if her actions result from the coherent set of desires with which she identifies (or would identify were she to think about it). Third, this theory can account for a person's identification with her desires (and beliefs). A person identifies (or would identify) with her desires insofar as she has authorized (or would authorize) them by both adopting them and ensuring that they are consistent with her coherent body of desires and beliefs.

This account of autonomy thus makes sense of the notion of a person as a self-determining being. It makes sense of a person as a self-determining being because it makes sense of how a person constitutes herself by gradually choosing (or abstaining to choose) her desires and beliefs in such a way as to form her character. This theory allows us to thus develop a theory of a person's character. A person's character is her relatively stable and coherent body of lower-order and higher-order desires and beliefs. It also allows a person's self to be identified as the holder of the character. A person then determines her own actions by producing actions that are (or can be) endorsed and effectuated by her character. A person is thus a being that is self-determining insofar as she shapes (or can shape) her self, character, and actions.

This account can also make sense of the intrinsic moral value to be attached to autonomy. The notion that this value tracks autonomy is, as I argue below, the best explanation of our beliefs with regard to a series of thought experiments. Also, if morality focuses on the good and the right, and if both the good for a person and the right treatment of him is at least in part a function of what he autonomously endorses, autonomy is going to be an important component of morality.[13] I am skeptical of the latter argument, because I suspect that it involves an unattractive type of moral relativism. However, a defense of this point is beyond the scope of this chapter.

Arguments against the notion of autonomy as a condition. The concept of autonomy might be thought to involve a set of capacities, such as the one I sketched earlier, or a condition whereby the agent actually determines her self, character, and actions through her evaluative processes.[14] An agent has the condition of autonomy only if she, through her own reasoning process, adopts certain desires and beliefs (both moral and nonmoral), initiates her projects on the basis of these desires and beliefs, and acts in a manner that is in general consistent with them. This process whereby the agent forms herself by authorizing certain desires and beliefs via other desires and beliefs (higher-order ones or ones that already form a coherent desire/belief set) occurs gradually and must begin with some externally imposed desires and beliefs (including some rules of rational reflection).[15] Also, this process may take into account both empirical considerations (e.g., the feelings of one's spouse) as well as abstract moral considerations (e.g., the duty to respect the dignity of others).[16] In short, the condition of autonomy consists in large part of the alignment of the first-order desires (and beliefs) and either the higher-order desires (or beliefs) or desires (or beliefs) that are stable and that already form a coherent desire/belief set. My claim is that the type of autonomy that grounds intrinsic moral value is autonomy as a capacity and not autonomy as a condition.

There are several reasons to favor the capacity notion. First, intuitively we attribute autonomy to a person with the relevant capacities even if he does not have some of the typical features of autonomy as a condition. For example, a man who simply adopts the moral views of the local moral authority and thereby adopts the views conventionally thought to be appropriate for his class or station, without any critical reflection on these views, fails to authenticate his moral views. This is one indicator that he does not have autonomy as a condition. If he regularly acts in a way that is inconsistent with these conventional moral views, then he may also have a lesser degree of integrity, another indicator that he has a lower level of autonomy as a condition. However, we would not judge such a person to be less than fully autonomous, thus suggesting that we view autonomy in the capacity sense.

Second, to the extent that we judge that moral responsibility presupposes autonomy and we judge that the above person is fully responsible for his actions, despite his reduced level of autonomy as a condition, we have another reason to view autonomy in the capacity sense.

Third, autonomy as a condition focuses on the alignment of first-order desires and beliefs and higher-order (or a coherent body of) desires and beliefs. This alignment may cease to exist where a person ceases to critically self-reflect on his first-order desires and beliefs. However, in the absence of mental illness, his autonomy does not seem to go in and out of existence. This invariance suggests that by autonomy we have in mind the capacity notion.[17]

Fourth, autonomy as a condition is a virtue. And it is not clear that the greater intrinsic moral value of persons over other beings is the result of their having greater virtue or perhaps their having the virtues in a more proper relation to each other. So, for example, where one could save either an evil person or a horse, it is not clear that the lack of virtue suffices to deprive the evil man of most of, let alone all of, his intrinsic moral value. In contrast, as I argue below, the loss of autonomy as a capacity would seem to eliminate most of, if not all of, the evil man's intrinsic moral value. This suggests that the type of autonomy that grounds the intrinsic moral value of persons is autonomy as a capacity.

Hence, the type of autonomy that corresponds to our ordinary sense of the property and that grounds the intrinsic moral value of persons is the capacity notion. More specifically, autonomy is the conjunction of (1) the capacity of an agent to choose on the basis of higher-order desires (and beliefs) with which she identifies which desires (and beliefs) guide her actions and thoughts and (2) the capacity to effectuate certain first-order desires (and beliefs) into action and thought.

Autonomy accounts for the relative intrinsic moral value of different types of beings. This notion of autonomy then helps account for intuitions about the relative intrinsic moral value of different types of beings. For example, if one is in a rescue boat and can save two cows or a fully functioning adult human being, the appropriate choice intuitively seems to be to save the human being. Similarly, if two human beings and a pig are stranded after a plane crash and will starve to death if one of the beings is not eaten, most persons find it intuitively preferable that the two human beings eat the pig. Intuitively, this seems a better result than straws being drawn with regard to who is to be eaten. This notion of the greater positive duty toward fully functioning human beings and the weaker duty toward the non-human animals can be explained in large part by differences in the intrinsic moral value of the two types of beings.

That instrumental values, for instance, beauty or financial value, cannot account for the aforementioned intuitions can be seen by modifying these thought experiments slightly. Imagine that in the above cases, the pigs have considerably more instrumental value than one of the persons (i.e., the drowning man in the first example and one of the starving men in the second). This might be the case if one of the persons has no close friends or family and is a financial drain on society due to a neurological disease that disrupts his motor skills. In contrast, the pig may have distinctive musculature that makes it very tasty, and as a result its ability to reproduce is greatly valued by consumers and manufacturers of pork products. Under such an assumption, our intuitions remain constant, thus suggesting that it is the relative intrinsic value of the beings and not their overall value that accounts for our judgments of these cases.

One main difference between a pig and a fully functioning adult that accounts for our intuitions in the aforementioned cases is a difference in mental capacity. This can be seen in that our intuitions with regard to this case fade if we imagine the pig having the same mental capacity as the adult human beings. Intuitively, a pig with a mind like ours ought to be treated like any other person. Other possible grounds of intrinsic moral value that are not linked to developed thought, such as the capacity to feel pleasure or pain and sentience, do not seem capable of distinguishing an ordinary pig from an adult human being.[18] Different grounds of intrinsic value, such as the capacity to live in complex and meaningful personal relations and the capacity to understand and act on moral duties, all seem to rest on differences relating to mental capacity and willing. In particular, I would suggest that the relevant attribute is autonomy, which includes not only the ability to self-consciously assess one's beliefs, desires, and actions but also a limited ability to shape these objects on the basis of the agent's assessment. This focus on autonomy captures the mental-capacity feature of the ground of intrinsic value. It also accounts for the close relation between beings who are intrinsically valuable and beings who are, under standard conditions, morally responsible for their actions.

One might object here that the intuitive preference for fully functioning human beings over pigs and other less intelligent beings is better explained by morally irrelevant factors than by differences in intrinsic moral value. The objector claims that it is the tendency of human beings to identify and empathize with their own species that explains the aforementioned preference, and that this deeply embedded preference is a function of factors, whether learned or genetic, that had and continue to have value in helping human beings survive. The objector's argument is further strengthened by the intuitive preference many people have for saving the lives of human beings who are suffering from an extreme degree of mental retardation over more intelligent animals (or aliens, in certain hypothetical situations). One response is that the intuitions here do not clearly favor one of the two competing views. While some human beings have intuitions favoring human beings over other non-human beings, regardless of the relative levels of autonomy, many others (such as myself) do not. A second and related response is that it seems possible to discount the intuitions favoring human beings qua biological species. In general, where a moral intuition reflects a morally arbitrary feature, it can be discounted, since the truth of the intuition is not likely the best explanation of why persons have it. In this case, since a significant intuitive difference rests on mere membership in a biological category, and since membership in a biologically category is a morally arbitrary feature, at least as a theoretical matter intuitions focusing on membership in that category ought to be discounted. However, the intuitive preference for fully functioning human beings is not subject to this same arbitrariness objection. In addition, it receives further support because it coheres with a wide range of intuitions concerning the good and the right.

One might further object that according to my view, we gain moral worth as we get older (assuming that we increase our intelligence), until the point when we start losing that capacity. This, the objector argues, is counterintuitive. For several reasons, the pattern of intuitions is not as clear as the objector claims. First, instrumental concerns are not easily screened out. It is hard to think of the value of children when they are not viewed as likely to develop into fully autonomous beings. Second, if a child has the same level of autonomy, or lack thereof, and intelligence as a non-human being (e.g., an ape), and we favor the interests of the former, this may reflect inappropriate considerations creeping into our judgments. Such considerations might include species favoritism, concerns for the autonomous being into which the child will likely develop, or concerns for the child's family members. Third, some persons, such as myself, do not find this conclusion the least bit counterintuitive, although I am not sure to what extent others share my intuitions.

The relevance of autonomy can also be seen in hypotheticals involving non-human persons. Imagine that there are extraterrestrial, non-human persons. Such beings have intelligence levels and a capacity to understand and act on moral duties that are similar to those of fully functioning human beings. Intuitively, and this can be seen in numerous science fiction movies, such persons seem to be almost as, if not as, intrinsically valuable as human persons.[19] This can be seen in that such non-human persons would seem to have similar rights and be subject to similar moral and legal duties as human persons. And, as in the earlier objection, intuitions to the contrary should probably be discounted as mistakenly tracking mere membership in a biological category. The unifying factor between fully functioning human persons and the aliens seems to be some combination of rationality and the ability to act on the basis of one's rational decisions (i.e., autonomy). Other features, such as a rich emotional life, may slightly increase the intrinsic value of a being, although it is not clear intuitively or otherwise that this should be the case.

Autonomy Is Proportional to Intelligence

Autonomy is in part a function of intelligence. Greater intelligence, which is a type of capacity, allows the agent to more effectively assess beliefs and desires. The agent's ability to assess the truth of her beliefs and the appropriateness of her desires is crucial if she is to be able to adopt views that truly reflect her own vision of her identity and to be able to escape the immediate forces operating on her. Also, greater intelligence allows for an increased ability to choose those first-order desires that will satisfy the second-order desires, thus allowing her to have a greater ability to align her desire/belief set and her actions. And the more intelligent an autonomous being is, the better able she is to ensure that she has a consistent and prioritized system of desires and beliefs. Without a consistent and prioritized desire/belief system, the second-order desires are going to be in tension and possibly inconsistent and thus will lessen the agent's ability to control her actions on the basis of self-chosen principles. Instead, the applicable second-order volitions will be a function of the most pressing external forces and not part of a prioritized and unified set of principles that is part of a person's identity. Note that the level of intelligence here affects autonomy as a capacity, insofar as it affects the two capacities that comprise autonomy. That the level of intelligence also affects autonomy as a condition is true but not part of my argument.[20]

My claim is that an increase in intelligence is closely related to, perhaps necessarily related to, the ability of an agent to assess her beliefs and desires, adopt a consistent and prioritized belief/desire set, and align her belief/desire set to her actions. My claim rests on the assumption that increased intelligence probably will produce an increased ability in a person to assess the truth of a belief, assess the moral and instrumental desirability of a desire, and assess the coherence of different desires and beliefs (particularly ones at different levels) and actions. To the degree that this assumption is plausible, then my claim is plausible. However, I am not sure how this assumption could be confirmed through scientific experimentation, especially given the abstract nature of the autonomy-as-capacity model and conceptual issues regarding the essential nature of intelligence. If intelligence essentially consists in part of the ability to determine if beliefs or desires are consistent, or whether beliefs are true, then the connection would be at least in part conceptual, and this part would be discoverable a priori.

One might object that it is intelligence itself and not autonomy that best explains our intuitive preferences in the aforementioned case. The objector might assert that at the very least I have not ruled out intelligence as the variable that best explains the intuitive preference in the cases discussed above. The first thing to note about this objection is that while it may weaken my account of the relation between autonomy and intrinsic moral value, it does not damage the overall argument. This is because, given intergroup differences in intelligence, my argument can proceed in an even more straightforward fashion when intelligence rather than autonomy is the ground of intergroup differences in intrinsic moral value.

However, the objection should probably be rejected. One reason to think that great weight should be attached to autonomy is that its parts include both freedom of the will (interpreted as the capacity of an agent to determine which first-order desires bring about her action) and (most likely) the necessary and sufficient conditions for moral responsibility. Since we attach great value to these features of a being, we ought to attach great weight to the overall structure that makes the two features possible and that relates them to each other. A second reason to think that it is autonomy that carries the weight relates to the explanation of another pattern of intuitions. Intelligence is a component of autonomy, hence, one cannot imagine an autonomous but nonintelligent being. However, one can imagine a being that is greatly intelligent but not autonomous, since a being can have a complex thought pattern and a rich emotional life without having any control over his thoughts, desires, or actions. To see this, imagine two types of beings. The first type consists of fully functioning adult human beings with both intelligence and autonomy. The second type consists of considerably more intelligent beings but ones without autonomy. This latter type can contemplate many of the great academic questions but cannot control their thoughts, desires, or actions. Nor are they capable of entering into relationships with others, since they cannot interact with others. In addition, members of the second type are unable to inhibit troubling or degrading thoughts about others, again, because of their lack of control over their mental life. Intuitively, a world with only the first type of beings is morally preferable (to a considerable degree) to a world with an equal number of only the second type, other things equal. One explanation for this intuition is that the former beings have greater intrinsic moral value, hence, that autonomy is a significant ground of intrinsic moral value.

Intrinsic Moral Value Is Not an All-or-Nothing Property

One might object that all persons are of equal intrinsic value, because autonomy is a mere threshold notion.[21] The idea here is that the intrinsic moral value that rests on autonomy is an all-or-nothing property that is maximally present once a being has a threshold level of autonomy. This notion conflicts with a general pattern with regard to the relation between an intrinsically morally valuable entity and the ground of its intrinsic moral value. In general, the following rule seems to apply to this relation: other things equal, the greater the amount of a ground of an intrinsically morally valuable entity, the more intrinsic moral value the entity has. For example, if a state of affairs is intrinsically morally good in virtue of its containing pleasure then, other things equal, a state of affairs with more pleasure has a greater amount of intrinsic moral goodness than an otherwise identical state of affairs containing less pleasure. A similar relation holds between states of affairs (or objects or events) whether the ground relates to a good conceptually independent of moral notions (e.g., pleasure) or a good conceptually dependent on them (e.g., a right action). In the absence of a reason to the contrary, we should assume that the pattern of grounding of intrinsic moral value in persons is similar.

The objector might claim that the quantity of intrinsic moral value is not always a function of the quantity of the ground of the intrinsic moral value. So, for example, a world with trillions of slightly autonomous beings in it is not obviously more valuable than one with only 1 million greatly autonomous beings. My approach, however, is neutral between the average and classical accounts of the intrinsic value of a state of affairs constituted by the existence of persons. On the average account, the value of the state of affairs is a function of the average intrinsic value of the persons in it, while on the classical account, it is a function of the sum of the intrinsic value of the persons in it. Whether my approach is committed to the latter account depends on the nature of the ground of intrinsic moral value. The plausible candidates for the ground include the instantiation of autonomy, the degree of instantiation of autonomy, the average degree of instantiation of autonomy, etc. My theory could even adopt a complex account whereby the value of an entity is not the same as the value of the sum of its parts but is rather a function of the relation between its parts.[22] The adoption of only some of these would commit my approach to the classical account.

The objector might assert that there is a dissimilarity that defeats the analogy between the intrinsic moral value of a state of affairs and a person. She might further assert that while the former is a matter of degree, the latter is not. There are two problems with this objection. First, talk about a person being intrinsically valuable is on some accounts better understood as referring to a state of affairs that obtains.[23] This is because it is not merely the concrete particular that is intrinsically valuable, nor the property in virtue of which the person is valuable, but some entity constituted by, or relating to, both entities and an instantiation relation. Along these lines, one might think that it is not pleasure that is intrinsically good, but rather it is the obtaining of a state of affairs in which a being experiences pleasure that is intrinsically good. Second, even if persons as well as states of affairs bear intrinsic value, there still does not seem to be a feature of one but not the other, which suggests that increased amounts of a property that is (or is part of) the ground of intrinsic moral value do not produce different amounts of intrinsic moral value.

There appear to be cases of beings of intermediate autonomy, not fully autonomous or non-autonomous. Some persons suffering from mental retardation appear to fit into this category. Such beings' hazy thought patterns, susceptibility to surrounding influences, and minimal grasp of abstract notions all suggest a sort of degenerate autonomy. This indicates that autonomy itself is a capacity that can be had in degrees. While the aforementioned threshold notion may allow autonomy to be a matter of degree with only a certain degree being sufficient to ground full intrinsic moral value for a person, it is hard to see why someone would accept this notion. None of the main metaphysical explanations of intrinsic moral value seem to support it.

On one account, freedom and autonomy presuppose the existence of intrinsic moral value. On this account, it is in part through the ability to consider reasons that persons are free and autonomous. Not all reasons can be solely instrumentally morally valuable, because there would then be no foundation of moral value. Hence, there must be intrinsically morally valuable things. However, on this account, it does not follow that intrinsic moral value must be present to the same degree in the intrinsically morally valuable things. This conclusion follows when this account is supplemented by a principle of sufficient reason of morality, that is, relevantly similar cases ought to be treated alike, only if one assumes that persons are relevantly similar with regard to the ground of intrinsic moral value, and this assumption begs the question.

On a second account, intrinsic value is the outcome of a hypothetical or an actual contract. However, hypothetical and actual contracts need not result in persons having equal intrinsic value, as can be seen in the disparity of bargaining positions that does or may accompany contract formation. The proponent of this ground of intrinsic value may object here that the disparate bargaining power of autonomous agents is unfair, but unless she has a reason other than the bargainers being equally intrinsically valuable, such an account is unsupported. And it is hard to see what further reason the contract theorist could provide. The introduction of notions such as fairness or exploitation to require a specific outcome for the relevant hypothetical contract would beg the question. This is because both notions are parasitic on pre-institutional moral entities, such as moral rights or desert, eliminating the force of a hypothetical-contract argument.

On a third account, the grounding relation between autonomy and intrinsic moral value is discovered by the inference-to-the-best-explanation procedure. My own view is that only this third account is defensible, but an argument in support of this is beyond the scope of this chapter. On this account, it seems likely that any conclusion as to whether persons are of equal intrinsic moral value is an inference to the best explanation of persons' beliefs and behavior.[24] However, it is not clear that the inference to the best explanation of our beliefs, especially our intuitions, and our behavior supports the notion that persons are of equal intrinsic moral value.

Hence, in virtue of their having different amounts of autonomy, persons probably have, other things being equal, different amounts of intrinsic moral value. In the next section, I argue that in virtue of their having different levels of per capita intelligence, the classes of whites and Asians have greater per capita autonomy than does the class of blacks.

WHITES AND ASIANS HAVE GREATER PER CAPITA INTELLIGENCE THAN BLACKS

In arguing for this claim, I am making a number of assumptions the defense of which is outside the scope of this book. Here my argument depends on a number of controversial assumptions.

1. There is such a thing as general intelligence.
2. IQ tests reliably measure general intelligence.
3. There are measurable differences in the IQ tests among the races.

If the reader rejects any of these assumptions, and I shall not defend them in this book, then the argument in this chapter should be rejected.

There is a significant difference, approximately a standard deviation, between the average performance of blacks and the average performance of whites and Asians on IQ tests.[25] This difference shows up on a range of tests. In addition, a person's score on these tests is relatively stable over her lifetime. These tests are thought to measure general intelligence rather than a narrow portion of intelligence. This intelligence has some predictive power; for example, it correlates to some extent with the frequency of out-of-wedlock births, participation in certain types of employment, and criminality.

An objector might assert here that the best psychological models support the notion that there are multiple types of intelligence rather than a single type.[26] Hence, while IQ tests may measure at most a few of these types of intelligence, they leave out other types. Furthermore, the objector might then claim that autonomy is in part a function of the properly weighted product of the different types of intelligence, of which only some are measured by IQ tests. If true, this defeats the aforementioned argument only if blacks have a greater degree of at least some of the types of intelligence not measured by the IQ test than do the other two groups. In the absence of evidence in support of this or reason to believe that counterbalancing areas of superior intelligence are had by blacks, this objection fails. If successful, however, this objection does weaken my argument considerably, since the main type of evidence is going to be a weaker measure of the properly weighted product of types of intelligence than it is of general intelligence.

It might also be objected that this difference in general intelligence is due to differences in environment, specifically, the lingering effects of racism and slavery or the effects of different sociocultural heritages, rather than genetic differences. However, the source of the difference does not matter as long as the difference between classes of persons is relatively stable over the relevant time frame, which for my purposes is a generation, and it appears to be.[27] For an individual, a lowered level of intelligence that results from environmental deprivation correlates with less autonomy, other things equal, every bit as much as a lowered level of intelligence that results from genetic factors.

The objector might respond that membership in a racial group is a function of arbitrary physical characteristics rather than genetic or cultural factors, and hence is not the sort of attribute that could reasonably be thought to indicate a difference in per capita intrinsic moral value. This objection misses the point. My claim is that the per capita differences in intelligence result in an other-things-equal per capita difference in intrinsic moral value. This claim is not dependent on the etiology of the per capita differences in intelligence. In particular, this claim is not dependent on whether the intergroup differences result from genetic differences, sociocultural differences, or merely an uneven but a random genetic pattern.

My argument is also not weakened by the observation that the intragroup variance in intelligence within a particular racial group exceeds the intergroup racial differences. That the intragroup difference with regard to the amount of an attribute is greater than the intergroup difference with regard to it does not entail that, in the absence of other relevant information, group membership is not a useful evidential indicator of the amount of that feature.

I argued previously that autonomy is in part a function of (and in some sense proportional to) intelligence. If two groups differ in their per capita intelligence and not with regard to other components of autonomy (e.g., control over one's actions), then the two groups differ with regard to their per capita amounts of autonomy.[28] For the reasons mentioned earlier, this results in an other-things-equal difference in per capita intrinsic moral value. Autonomy-based differences in intrinsic moral value might still be offset by differences in other grounds of intrinsic moral value, which would then result in the different racial groups having equal amounts of per capita intrinsic moral value. In the next section, I argue that in the previously discussed racial groups, there probably are no such offsetting factors.

Other Factors Do Not Offset the Autonomy-Based Differences in Per Capita Intrinsic Moral Value

There are other plausible grounds for intrinsic moral value in persons: the feeling of pleasure and pain, moral goodness (i.e., the moral nature of one's character and acts), rationality, the capacity to enter into meaningful relationships with other persons or God, and the capacity to be aware of beauty. All of these grounds are not, as far as I can tell, present to a lesser degree in whites and Asians. In fact, with regard to at least one of these factors (e.g., moral goodness), differences in per capita amounts probably favor whites and Asians. This conclusion rests on the following two points: the greater frequency of involvement in crime by blacks, especially violent crime, and the assumption that in general an agent's performance of acts of illegal violence is morally wrong and reflects a flawed moral character.[29] Hence, the other-things-equal difference in per capita intrinsic moral value that accompanies differences in per capita autonomy apparently will not be offset by other grounds of intrinsic moral value in persons. Therefore, it follows that all things considered, blacks have less per capita intrinsic value than do whites and Asians.

PART 3
Implications of the Argument

The Per Capita Differences in the Context of an Array of Moral Considerations

The above conclusion is shocking. However, there are several reasons that weaken its impact.

First, if one is a nonconsequentialist, and I believe that one should be, then the right action is not always that action that brings about the state of affairs with the most intrinsic moral value. It does intuitively seem to be the case that the pleasure and desire-satisfaction of beings of greater intrinsic moral value are more valuable than the pleasure and desire-satisfaction of beings of less intrinsic moral value. However, there may still be defeasible side constraints on the treatment of persons (i.e., moral duties that restrain us from acting in certain ways toward persons), no matter what their level of intrinsic moral value. An example of such a side constraint might be the requirement that autonomous beings not be treated as though they are merely of instrumental value (e.g., they may not be used for food). Thus while it may bring about a better state of affairs to promote the interests of beings of greater intrinsic moral value rather than to respect side constraints on the treatment of beings of lesser intrinsic moral value, it does not follow that the latter can be sacrificed for the former.

Second, from the existence of intergroup differences in per capita intrinsic value, not much of importance follows with regard to the intrinsic moral value of each member of that group. In general, it does not follow from the fact that a class has an attribute that an individual member of that class has that attribute. In this case, there is great intragroup variance in the intelligence of any racial group and considerable overlap in the distribution of intelligence of different racial and ethnic groups. Hence, the differences in per capita autonomy-based intrinsic value will not result in a strong conclusion with regard to the relative intrinsic moral value of two members of different racial groups.

Third, there may be all-things-considered instrumental reasons to judge persons as individuals and leave out (or at least greatly discount the information to ignore for all practical purposes) the relevant statistical information about expected intrinsic moral value. One reason for this is that focusing on racial classification may in some contexts lead to a relatively inaccurate estimation of a person's intelligence. In general, where further information becomes available and negates the practical usefulness of racial or ethnic group-based characteristics, it is rational to disregard these characteristics. Another instrumental reason against using such information is that the use of the information may lead to resentment, hostility, or even violence from the persons who are members of groups that are (or feel that they are) shut out of educational and employment opportunities. It may also lead to an increased balkanization of the population and may further transform a somewhat principled distribution of resources into a group spoils system perhaps via further government incursion into the free market.

Significant Implications of the Per Capita Differences

Some significant implications follow from the per capita differences. One is that when it comes to positive duties owed to persons who have a general positive right against the agent, race as an indicator of intrinsic moral value may become relevant in shaping the agent's all-things-considered obligations. To see this, we must make a few distinctions with regard to rights. A positive right is a right that the duty holder perform an act of a certain kind, whereas a negative right is a right that the duty holder omit from acting in certain ways. A special right is a right that is grounded upon the performance of a particular act type (e.g., having signed a contract), a special relation (e.g., a parental relation), or the causing of harm. A general right is a right that is not a special right and that generally rests on a right holder's status as a person, an autonomous being, a sentient being, etc. If there are any positive general rights, and this is not obvious, then with regard to a particular interest type, the strength of the right is probably in part a function of the intrinsic value of the right holder. Consider first the pattern of intuitions that occurs with regard to negative general rights. Imagine that in the midst of a crowded farm show, a farmer discovers that in a pressurized container of hydrochloric acid he is holding that there is a hole, and within moments it will begin to spray a painful and blinding chemical substance. Given the crowded nature of his location, he must spray the substance either upward, which will blind and painfully mar three persons, or spray downward, which will blind and painfully mar three pigs. Both the persons and pigs seem to have a right not to be harmed, and being blinded and painfully marred by the unjustifiable spraying of a substance is a harming. Intuitively, the farmer is all-things-considered obligated to violate the rights of the pigs and not those of the persons. The best explanation of this intuition, and others with regard to similar situations, is that the strength of general rights is in part a function of the intrinsic moral value of the right holder. Next consider positive general rights. For example, imagine that a transplant surgeon can take the heart valve of a newly dead pig and use it to save the life of a chimpanzee or a fully functioning non-malevolent adult human being. Intuitively, it seems that the surgeon ought to favor the second. This is largely explained by the latter's greater intrinsic moral value. I claim that this pattern of intuitions also holds where the decision is between saving a severely retarded human being and a fully functioning one, although it is not clear to what extent others have the same intuitions. The best explanation of the general pattern of intuitions with regard to the relative strength of general rights, both positive and negative, is that the strength of the right is in part a function of the intrinsic moral value of the right holder. Since race and ethnicity are evidential indicators of intrinsic moral value, they are evidential indicators of the strength of a general right.

The praiseworthiness of a supererogatory act also is in part a function of the intrinsic moral value of the act's beneficiary. A supererogatory act has two essential elements: it is not obligatory and its agent is praiseworthy in virtue of having done it. The most likely explanation for the praiseworthiness of an agent who performs a supererogatory act is that the act is (or the act's results are) morally valuable and that persons are to be praised for intentionally doing acts that are (or that bring about results that are) morally valuable. This is especially true where the acts are done out of a limited range of motives. On this account, the moral value of a supererogatory action and the praiseworthiness of the agent for performing it are in part a function of the intrinsic moral value that it brings about. Since it is better, other things being equal, to bring about good things for beings with greater intrinsic moral value than lesser intrinsic moral value, the praiseworthiness of a supererogatory action is in part a function of the intrinsic moral value of the act's beneficiary.

The strength of a general right such as the praiseworthiness of a supererogatory act is in part a function of the intrinsic moral value of the recipient. To the extent that the United States has non-contractual policies designed to provide aid to non-citizens, and to the extent that it does not help everyone it could, it must either infringe upon some general rights or else not perform some supererogatory acts that are within its power. In either case, it seems preferable, although in the second case not obligatory, to act to help the more valuable beings. And for this, race and ethnicity are useful indicators. Such a policy would allow race and ethnicity to play an evidential role in deciding which groups should receive U.S. aid (e.g., whether the United States should save Albanians endangered by a civil war in Serbia or Tutsis endangered by a civil war in Rwanda). It should, however, be noted that there are other relevant and usually far weightier considerations (e.g., the number of persons involved).

A related implication of this argument is that it provides a moral reason to legalize race-based and ethnicity-based discrimination. There are two assumptions underlying this inference. First, the satisfaction of the interests of persons who are of greater intrinsic moral value is other things equal of greater value than the satisfaction of the interests of persons of lesser intrinsic moral value. This assumption is intuitively appealing when making a comparison of the value of interest satisfaction between species (e.g., between human beings and pigs). Second, there is a moral reason to permit persons to bring about more valuable states of affairs. Combining these two ideas, we end up with the claim that there is a moral reason to permit discrimination. Now, of course, this moral reason may be exceedingly weak and other moral concerns (e.g., efficiency and perhaps fairness) may weigh against permitting such a shift.

In the absence of evidence of the intelligence or other grounds of intrinsic moral value about potential beneficiaries of a person's action, this reasoning indicates that there is a moral reason for private parties to discriminate in favor of whites and Asians over blacks. Once again, there are two background assumptions here. First, the satisfaction of the interests of persons who are of greater intrinsic moral value is other things equal of greater moral value than the satisfaction of the interests of persons of lesser intrinsic moral value. Second, persons have an other-things-equal moral reason to bring about more valuable states of affairs. Also, the usual caveats apply, namely, that the absence of relevant evidence may be a condition that is not often satisfied and that other considerations may override this moral reason. Nonetheless, this reason applies in some cases to a wide range of private decisions. For example, it follows that race is a relevant factor in deciding which philanthropic organizations to support, which person to employ, and whom to help through charitable acts. The weight to be given to such considerations is a topic that requires a different and in part a fact-intensive analysis that is beyond the scope of this chapter.

PART 4
Conclusion

There are differences in the measured levels of IQ between different racial groups. Insofar as these scores measure general intelligence and insofar as autonomy is in part a function of intelligence, there are, other things being equal, differences in the per capita level of autonomy between racial groups. Since autonomy is a ground of intrinsic moral value and since the per capita differences are not offset by other factors, there are per capita differences in the intrinsic moral value of racial groups. Thus insofar as an agent must choose between satisfying competing general rights or between performing mutually exclusive supererogatory duties, there is a moral reason to take the race of potential beneficiaries of her action into account.

If members of historically oppressed groups do not have a right to compensation, strong affirmative action, or reparations for slavery, then the failure to provide such benefits is not unjust unless it fails to express their moral worth. I argued earlier that with at least one such group, blacks, the failure to express their equal moral worth is not unjust because they do not have equal value understood in terms of their per capita intrinsic moral value. The failure to provide such benefits might still not express their proper moral worth if it underestimates their moral worth without claiming that it is of equal value. However, it is not clear that the failure to provide such benefits expresses any such message. All that such a failure probably expresses is the notion that persons' property rights and freely acquired wealth should not be disrupted on behalf of vague expressions of respect. Even the notion that the Kantian imperative is to be understood in terms of the duty to express certain ideas is questionable. I would argue that expression is merely instrumentally valuable and that the duty prevents the violation of specific rights since they provide the constraints of (and perhaps requirements of) treatment that respects the dignity of persons as autonomous beings.

SECTION 6

Educational Diversity

7

Experiential Diversity

In this book, I argued that affirmative action and reparations are not justified on compensatory grounds. My project is somewhat disconnected from the real-world debate, especially the legal debate, which has focused largely on the forward-looking grounds, especially educational diversity. For example, I have not spent any time discussing the arguments found in recent court cases on affirmative action. This is explained by the purpose of the book, which is to investigate the backward-looking arguments for affirmative action and reparations. In this chapter I assess the dominant legal argument for affirmative action in colleges and universities and then relate it to the backward-looking arguments that are the focus of this book.

This year the Supreme Court will face the issue of whether preferential treatment for minorities is consistent with the Equal Protection Clause. This chapter explores the diversity justification of such programs, both because it lies at the heart of the constitutional issue that the Court will face, and because it is one of the most widely invoked justifications for these programs. The analysis of this justification is in part legal and in part moral. It is in part legal because previous cases have narrowed the type of diversity that may be used to justify such programs, and in part moral because the notion that a state has a compelling interest in diversity is partially a moral one.

This chapter focuses on a recent case involving preferential treatment at the University of Michigan School of Law because it is the most recent case on this topic and the one likely to go to the Supreme Court. The next part of the chapter involves an evaluation of the Court's approach to diversity. The argument here is that the sort of diversity rationale that schools such as Michigan rely on is intertwined with a concern for truth, but that such a concern undermines the minority-experience rationale for preferential treatment. The last part of this chapter provides and discusses an approach to diversity that is more general than that which lies at the heart of the legal issue.

PART 1
Grutter and *Bakke*

On May 14, in *Grutter v. Bollinger* (2002), the proponents of preferential treatment won a big legal battle. In explaining this victory, it is helpful to revisit the Supreme Court's decision in *Regents of California v. Bakke* (1978), which shaped the *Grutter* decision. In *Bakke,* the Supreme Court considered the constitutional status of the preferential treatment plan used by the University of California-Davis Medical School. In a highly competitive context (there were 3,000 applicants for 100 slots), the school set aside sixteen of the slots for minorities. Alan Bakke, a white man who was rejected by the medical school, sued, claiming that his rejection in favor of less qualified minorities ran afoul of the Equal Protection Clause and Title VI of the 1964 Civil Rights Act. The Supreme Court split into three blocks. A liberal block of four held that the Constitution and Title VI permitted such benign quotas and that Davis's plan was therefore constitutional. A second block of four held that the program was illegal, since it violated the plain language of Title VI. This left Justice Louis Powell with the decisive vote. His reasoning has generally become associated with the case and is frequently cited in support of the notion that such programs are constitutional.

Powell argued that racially discriminatory policies should receive "strict scrutiny," a test that requires that the state's goal be a compelling one and that its discriminatory policy be narrowly tailored to achieve that goal. He argued that because student diversity in life experiences contributes to classroom learning in other students, it is a compelling state goal, hence, race may be considered a plus factor for minority applicants. However, he then noted that Davis's quota system was not narrowly tailored to this goal, since it could have been achieved by a system that gave applicants individual consideration. Powell contrasted Davis's quota system with one that gave applicants individualized consideration by treating diversity as merely one of many factors in the admissions process and that allowed each applicant to compete for all of the slots. Powell held that individualized consideration of applicants takes into account each applicant's combined attributes. His examples of relevant attributes include those such as compassion, a history of overcoming disadvantage, and an ability to communicate with the poor. Thus, on Powell's account, Davis's plan failed strict scrutiny. Along the way, he rejected an argument that preferential treatment was justified as a way to rectify past injustices, holding that such an argument required a specific showing of past injustices by the institution in question.

In *Grutter*, the University of Michigan Law School, one of the best in the country, adopted a system that gave significant weight to members of certain minority groups (the usual suspects: African Americans, Hispanics, and Native Americans). The program it adopted in effect automatically admitted favored minorities for grades and standardized test (LSAT) scores that for whites and Asians would nearly always result in rejection. One example of the difference is that if we hold the standardized test (LSAT) score constant, minorities with a high C to a low B undergraduate average were admitted at the same rate as majority applicants with an A average. The law school conceded that 3 out of 4 minority students would not be admitted if applications were considered in a color-blind manner. The majority in *Grutter* found such a policy constitutional. Their reasoning had two parts. First, they were bound to follow Powell's guidelines. Second, the law school's policy satisfied those guidelines. The Court, following Powell, found that educational diversity is a compelling state goal and that Michigan's system was narrowly tailored to achieve this goal, since it gave applicants individualized consideration.

The dissent in *Grutter* rejected a number of premises in the majority's argument. They rejected the notion that Powell's opinion bound them, on two grounds. First, his opinion did not receive the support of a majority of justices in either *Bakke* or later Supreme Court cases. Second, even if this were not the case, his guidelines were not binding, since they were not essential to his argument in support of Alan Bakke's claim.

The dissent then argued that diversity is not a compelling state goal. The Court notes that diversity of experiences would support positive discrimination against vastly overrepresented groups (e.g., Jews) and favoritism to be shown to persons with the most unique experiences (e.g., professional jazz musicians).

They also argued, and this is significant for the purposes of this chapter, that Michigan's admissions system was not narrowly tailored to achieve experiential diversity. They claimed that such an attempt would have to take into account the range of ways that any one individual might contribute to diversity. For instance, they noted that the school gave preference to a black graduate of Choate and Harvard over a poor, rural white applicant and questioned whether the black really contributed more to campus diversity. Instead, Michigan appeared to be assuming that each minority applicant would likely make a great contribution to diversity and that each non-minority applicant would likely make little to no contribution. This contention was supported by the fact that despite its claim to the contrary, Michigan appeared to be using a quota system. For example, between 1995 and 1998, the last four years for which data were available, the law school enrolled minorities at a rate of 13.5 to 13.7 percent of the class.[1]

There is now a clear split in the federal appellate courts. The Ninth and Sixth Circuits have held that they are bound by *Bakke* and that preferential treatment is constitutional. The Fifth Circuit has taken the opposite view. The Eleventh Circuit ducked the issue of whether state colleges and universities have a compelling interest in diversity but held that even if they do, race may not be used as a proxy for it. This split will almost undoubtedly force the Supreme Court to face this issue.

PART 2
Experiential Diversity and Truth

For opponents of preferential treatment, it is worthwhile stepping back and considering why the diversity rationale should be rejected. As the dissent points out, the law school really sought to protect slots for blacks and Hispanics rather than seeking true intellectual or experiential diversity. The latter goals favor the entry of Marxists, fundamentalist Christians, Afghans, convicted rapists, primitive tribesmen, and transsexuals, since such persons likely have ideas and experiences that differ sharply from white students who recently graduated near the top of their Ivy League class. Instead, the law school focused on admitting minority students who usually have the same ideas and sometimes the same experiences as their upper-class white peers.

The more interesting issue here is whether such a program could be more narrowly tailored toward such a goal. Consider the three things that the experiences of less talented minority applicants might be thought to add to a classroom.[2] First, they might contribute to the class's gaining an understanding of their group's beliefs (e.g., why do blacks overwhelmingly favor big government?). Second, they might contribute to an understanding of things other than the group's beliefs (e.g., when it comes to court costs, whether we should adopt a loser-pays rule). Third, they might get other members of the class to adopt their beliefs. The second justification is dubious. Let us assume that the favored minorities are more skeptical about authority, distrust others' motives, and have firsthand experience with discrimination. It is hard to see how this will likely contribute to subtle issues in unrelated areas such as corporate law. In fact, given the lesser abilities of the minority applicants (as evidenced by their lower scores), one would expect that they would contribute less to the exploration of such issues than would other applicants.

In general, the value of learning about or adopting a group's beliefs depends at least in part on the likelihood that these beliefs are true. In part, this explains why law schools are not interested in giving diversity-based preference to convicted drug dealers, conspiracy theorists, or fundamentalist

Christians. The universities believe that such groups' beliefs are likely false, hence, not particularly worthy of discussion or adoption. Moreover, this value is considerably less important for places such as math programs and medical schools, where the beliefs in question are largely irrelevant to the course of study.[3]

The colleges and universities are on solid ground in being concerned with the contribution to knowledge by any underrepresented group, for if the value of education is tightly linked to the promotion of knowledge, then this goal is likely hindered by the introduction of less able students who are distinguished by the fact that they hold false or poorly defended beliefs. Nor should persons who deny that the value of education rests on objective knowledge, perhaps because they do not think that such knowledge exists, reject this type of argument. This is because an analogous argument likely works for a justification of education on the basis of its contribution to rationality, overall well-being, justice, communal flourishing, etc.

What are the beliefs of favored minorities in the context of a university? This is not clear, but there appear to be three that often receive public recognition. First, justice is egalitarian (i.e., concerned with equality). Second, with regard to certain minorities (e.g., blacks, Hispanics, the poor), these claims of justice have been and are frequently trampled upon. Third, the government has a far-reaching mandate to aggressively combat this injustice. If we view these beliefs as controversial and not obviously worthy of promotion, then the case for this type of experiential diversity weakens considerably. This objection is distinct from one based on the dishonest way in which colleges and universities pursue experiential diversity.

If this is correct, then the strength of the learning-from-the-oppressed argument for preferential treatment rests on the truth or falsity of the experiential insights had by blacks, Hispanics, etc. The three beliefs are likely false. Obviously, an in-depth discussion of them is outside the scope of this chapter, however, a sketch of a few of the reasons to oppose the first two beliefs might be helpful since it undercuts the case for favoring diversity that leads to the promotion of these beliefs.

First, justice is not egalitarian. Often the concern for equality is understood in terms of equal treatment, which in turn is cashed out in terms of treatment that is a fitting response to various attributes (e.g., interest, moral autonomy, and desert). The role of equality can come in via the selection of the basic principles of justice or at a less abstract level, where it grounds constraints on the way in which persons are treated in different spheres (e.g., work, medical treatment, and political influence). However, the value of equality reflects an underlying metaphysical or political starting point, such as the fact that all persons are equally autonomous, or that their interests are equally valuable. Establishing the falsity of a broad class of theories is obviously beyond the scope of this chapter; nonetheless, it is useful to indicate the strategy of criticism that critics of egalitarian justice employ. To the extent that equality relates to an attribute of a person, it is hard to find an attribute that all persons have in equal degree. Persons differ in their merit, desert, intelligence, rationality, autonomy, and virtue. They even differ in their moral autonomy, since they vary in the degree to which they can come to understand, accept, and act on various moral principles. The egalitarian might claim that persons are alike in virtue of their equal degrees of personhood. The problem with this claim is in identifying an attribute, distinct from the aforementioned ones, that is both the defining characteristic of personhood and that grounds value in the person.

Second, consider the notion that but for slavery or past discrimination, blacks would have the same income and distribution of positions as whites. This notion appears to be present in the penumbra of the three beliefs and in the resulting notion that the state has a mandate to reduce inequality between the races. This notion cannot account for the evidence that there are genetic differences in the average intelligence of racial groups and that such differences will likely affect the groups' comparative economic performance.[4] Also, it also runs against the idea that there are probably differences in sociocultural beliefs, attitudes, and values between different groups.[5] While not genetic, these are deeply embedded factors that are also likely to affect a group's economic performance. There are also destructive behaviors that are not the result of discrimination and that likely produce inequality between racial groups. For example, in the mid-1990s, blacks had nearly a 70 percent out-of-wedlock birthrate.[6] Since out-of-wedlock births are associated with many destructive behaviors (e.g., crime), attitudes and activity leading to out-of-wedlock births have harmful effects on the black community. Blacks also commit a disproportionately large amount of violent crimes. For example, during recent periods, they have constituted 50 to 60 percent of the arrests for murders and 50 percent of the arrests for rape (and these rates match the frequency distribution of victims' reports).[7] Out-of-wedlock births and violent crimes are, in general, voluntary acts for which moral responsibility rests on the agent who performs them. When such acts form a general pattern in the black community, they produce an unequal distribution of income and wealth when compared to other racial groups.

One objection likely to arise here is that the differences in intelligence, sociocultural beliefs and values, crime rates, etc. between the descendants of slaves and other U.S. populations are the effects of slavery and related oppression (e.g., segregation and widespread racism). This claim is not obvious. For example, interracial adoption studies provide evidence that there is a genetic explanation of interracial differences in intelligence.[8] If intelligence affects such things as poverty, schooling, welfare dependency, parenting, and crime, then there is a non-discriminatory explanation of some of the interracial differences in these areas.[9] However, even if these genetic explanations fail, we think that many persons, even ones from rotten social backgrounds, are morally responsible for a good deal of their acts, despite the etiology of these actions. If this is correct, then it further seems that a person may not collect for harmful or self-destructive behavior for which he is fully responsible. To see this, consider the case: *hothead.*

> A man gets his car dented due to another driver's negligence. As a result of his anger over the accident, he gives his wife a severe beating, thereby grounding a just claim in her that he be punished. It intuitively seems that the negligent driver may not be made to pay the husband's debt to his wife, despite the driver's having caused her injury.

Let us set aside what accounts for this result, for example, intervention by a morally responsible agent, the unforeseeability of this result, the limited scope of the driver's duty, or the lack of proximate causation. Any blanket denial of responsibility would undercut blacks' and other minorities' degree of moral responsibility, a claim that can hardly fit into an argument for current equality between the races.

If these beliefs are false, then preferential treatment designed to bring in persons with such beliefs seems to defeat a major educational purpose: to encourage true beliefs. Even if the beliefs are merely controversial, it is hard to see why they should be promoted via preferential treatment if they are already far more prevalent than the competitor set of beliefs. For example, the majority of students at the University of Michigan School of Law probably accept these beliefs. This is almost certainly true with regard to the majority of faculty.[10] If this principle is correct, then the argument from experiential diversity seems incapable of supporting preferential treatment for blacks, Hispanics, and Native Americans.

An objector might provide a number of reasons to challenge the notion that the concern for diversity ought to be understood as diversity among true or likely true beliefs. First, it is often hard to identify which beliefs are true. Second, we have good reason to withhold from any university official the power to pronounce decisively which are the true ones, or if the university official is to make pronouncements via her admission decisions she ought to focus on justification rather than truth. Third, for purposes of social comity, we do better to aim at acknowledging and considering beliefs under the category of reasonable rather than true. Fourth, for Millian reasons, there may be benefits to providing a forum for false beliefs.

In arguing for the value of introducing certain ideas, the colleges and universities are arguing that there is value in promulgating these ideas. This value is grounded in different features of a belief, most likely its truth, justification, relation to knowledge, or its causal effects on a population's well-being. Truth is related to the first three of these grounds, since justification is probably best understood as truth conducivity, and knowledge has a truth requirement. In addition, whether a belief will have certain causal effects on a population's well-being often depends on whether it is true. For example, whether a belief about the effectiveness of a particular treatment for AIDS has a desirable effect on AIDS patients depends at least in part on whether that belief is true. The value of truth (or truth-related states, e.g., knowledge) also in part explains why universities prefer students who perform better in classes. If the value of truth helps justify the value of having universities and selecting certain types of students to attend, then it is likely valuable for university officials to make judgments about which beliefs (or broad classes of them) warrant pursuit via the admissions process. Where our beliefs about which beliefs are true are unjustified and known to be so, the officials ought not to make such judgments, because they will not be reliably promoting these truth-related values. However, where we do have adequate justification of which beliefs (or classes of them) are true, then labeling them "reasonable" rather than "true" is dishonest and also runs the risk of decreasing the accuracy with which the relevant judgments are made.

There is value in having a forum for false beliefs, but this value rests on the value of having true (or justified or knowledge-related) mental states and that the forum will likely be present even where there is an attempt to screen out false beliefs. This is because given the number and variety of plausible well-defended views and the incentives for students and faculty to introduce these ideas, the forum by which false ideas are introduced and discussed will flourish. The underlying assumption here is that universities that do not select for merit are not likely to have a better marketplace of ideas. Related to this assumption is the notion that the merit-based criterion relates to students' knowledge-based abilities or accomplishments.

PART 3
A More General Approach to Diversity

In deciding which experiences or ideas, if any, warrant preferential treatment, the courts should have adopted a broader set of principles. Here is a principle that might be relevant for law schools.

> (1) Other things being equal, beliefs or experiences ought to be considered a plus factor in a law school applicant's favor only if relative to his most meritorious replacement the applicant's beliefs or experiences will improve his or his classmates' legal reasoning (including certain knowledge components) or law-related performance.

Lawyering ability may be a mere instrument by which to achieve other values (e.g., justice, utility, or the protection of a Christian community). The idea behind (1) is that in the context of law school, the main purpose of admitting one applicant over another is to produce a person who is a better lawyer, does better things with his law degree, or contributes more to his classmates than his likely replacement. The replacement in this context is the one who would prevail in a system unconcerned with diversity. Analogous principles can be put forth for undergraduate liberal arts programs, medical schools, dental schools, etc. The issue then arises whether black, Hispanic, and Native American applicants are better than the applicants who were rejected because of a preferential system or whether the minority applicants contribute more to their classmates. This type of broad-based argument is set out in a highly influential defense of preferential treatment.[11] However, as noted earlier, the courts narrow the constitutional debate to a discussion of whether preferential treatment leads to educational benefits for classmates of "diverse" students.

This broader argument is more powerful than the narrow argument, since it opens the door for arguments based on minority contributions as role models, doctors and lawyers in poor communities, political activists, etc. In the context of the academy, it allows for arguments based on minority ability to contribute to research as well as student learning. And it allows for arguments based on the value of promoting equal opportunity. However, such general diversity arguments appear to override some claim of white male applicants. For the purposes of this chapter, we need not address the issue of whether the white applicant's claim is based on a more general claim to equal treatment, the general demands of justice, his greater educational interest, or his greater moral desert.[12] Given this override, the proponent of preferential treatment has the burden to establish that the diversity-related benefits override the negative consequences of preferential treatment. These include: efficiency losses accompanying the selection of less talented persons, resentment on behalf of the most qualified applicant (where diversity is set aside), the stigmatization of black and Hispanic students, increased failure in these students, and the balkanization that occurs where groups compete for state-distributed resources.[13] It is unlikely that such a showing can be made, but at the very least the consideration of policy would not exclude morally relevant consequences from consideration.

As a legal matter, it might be argued that these are the sort of policy considerations that are more appropriate for a legislature than a judiciary. On some accounts of statutory interpretation, moral principles are either irrelevant or relevant but limited to principles of justice rather than the balance of consequentialist considerations. And if these broader consequentialist considerations are irrelevant to the constitutional status of preferential treatment, then the narrower policy considerations that characterized the experiential diversity argument are as well.[14]

PART 4
Equal-Opportunity Arguments

While the courts have relied on diversity arguments for affirmative action, there are a number of other purportedly forward-looking arguments given in support of these programs. Some of these are in fact covert backward-looking arguments. Equal-opportunity arguments are often prime examples of this. These arguments defend such programs on the grounds that they eliminate those hindrances to opportunity that involve or are the result of injustice. Those hindrances to opportunity that result from genetics, family structure, culture, or liberty are often thought to be immune to legal interference. The concern to eliminate the effects of past injustice is the hallmark of a backward-looking argument.

Even if this were not the case, equal opportunity is a vague notion. If we interpret opportunity in terms of probability, then a competitor's overall employment opportunity is the graph of his probability of getting a job plotted against all currently available jobs. Given that persons have different preferences, we might then say that the value of a person's employment opportunity is the sum of his chances at the different jobs weighted to reflect normative considerations.[15] These considerations might reflect the person's preferences, the likelihood of different jobs satisfying his interests, his moral character, etc. Equality of opportunity obtains when classes of persons have identically valued employment opportunities. Sufficient opportunity would occur when most or all persons have employment opportunities whose value exceeds a particular threshold.

The problem with the two types of opportunity relations arises when we try to identify the relevant classes by which we determine what opportunities particular individuals should have. That is, the opportunity theorist needs to identify which factors go into specifying the relevant classes. For example, it is unclear which of the following factors are ones that should identify the relevant classes: genetic capacities, family structure, cultural background, and market imperfections. The issue of class identification gets rather complex, since some of the factors might themselves have resulted from injustices in the distant past and yet at the same time be factors that are essential to a person's identity (e.g., his genetic makeup), whereas others, with a similar history, are central to his psychological makeup (e.g., his job and mate preferences). In such a case, it becomes unclear whether it is coherent to think that such a person has a claim to increased opportunity based on the competition-hindering effects of these factors.

Even if such an account can be coherently set out, it is unclear whether either equal or sufficient opportunity is desirable. Equalizing or transferring opportunity might be wrong because it would require enormous losses in liberty and efficiency. This will occur because of the transfer of resources or invasion into private realms that is necessary to counteract the competitive advantages of certain families and sociocultural values.[16] The opportunity goals are themselves not obviously morally good if one thinks that opportunities or well-being should track persons' desert or not fit into any pattern.[17] I will assert but not defend that both criticisms of opportunity programs are sound, since a defense of them will take us far afield.

PART 5
Conclusion

In *Grutter*, preferential treatment was held to be constitutional on the basis of the contribution of "diverse" students to the education of their classmates. An implicit assumption in this argument, at least given how schools such as Michigan have interpreted it, is that the contribution involves making it more likely that the other students adopt the beliefs (or perspective) of the minorities. Three beliefs seem relevant here: justice is concerned with equality, racial and ethnic minorities are currently treated unequally, and the state has a mandate to combat this type of injustice. The first two beliefs are likely false, and in any case they are already well represented on campuses. If these arguments succeed, then this narrow experiential diversity argument is incapable of establishing the moral permissibility, let alone the constitutionality, of these programs. A broader consequentialist argument may avoid this objection, but only at the extent of introducing constitutionally irrelevant considerations.

Notes

INTRODUCTION

1. See Thomas Sowell, *Inside American Education* (New York: The Free Press, 1993), citing Geoff Henley, "Unequal Justice under Law School," *The Daily Texan* (University of Texas-Austin), April 3, 1991, p. 4. The University of Texas policy was held by the Fifth Circuit to be unconstitutional. See *Hopwood v. Texas,* 78 F. 3d 932 (5th Cir. 1996).

2. See Herrnstein and Charles Murray, *The Bell Curve* (New York: The Free Press, 1994), 451–55, citing *COFHE Admissions Statistics: Classes Entering 1991 and 1992 (Redbook XVII)* (Cambridge: Consortium on Financing Higher Education, 1992), Appendix D. The authors looked at twenty-six of the nation's elite schools, including sixteen of the twenty top-rated private universities and five of the top-ten private colleges as ranked in "Best Colleges," *U.S. News and World Report* (October 4, 1993): 107–27.

3. See James Crouse and Dale Trusheim, *The Case against the SAT* (Chicago: University of Chicago Press, 1988), 96–98.

4. See Herrnstein and Murray, *The Bell Curve,* 455–56.

5. Ibid., 456–57.

6. The first three examples are cited in Dinesh D'Souza, *The End of Racism* (New York: The Free Press, 1995), 67–69.

7. See "Tax Report," *Wall Street Journal,* October 19, 1994, p. A1; Marsha Ginsburg, "Slavery Payback Is Only a Dream," *Washington Times,* October 23, 1994, p. A5.

8. The activist's views are cited in Richard F. America, ed., *The Wealth of Races: The Present Value of Benefits from Past Injustices* (New York: Greenwood Press, 1990), 100.

9. See Bernard Boxill, *Blacks and Social Justice* (Lanham: Rowman & Littlefield, 1992), 36.

Chapter 1. The Most Qualified Applicant

1. Title VII of the 1964 Civil Rights Act was justified in part on the basis of merit. For example, one of its sponsors, Senator Hubert Humphrey, stated "In Title VII we seek to prevent discriminatory hiring practices. We seek to give people an opportunity to be hired on the basis of merit" (110 *Cong. Rec.* 6549 [1964]). Congressman Joseph Minish stated that "Under Title VII, employment will be on the basis of merit, not race" (110 *Cong. Rec.* 1600 [1964]). Senator Joseph Clark (along with Humphrey) wrote that "[T]he very purpose of Title VII is to promote hiring on the basis of job qualifications, rather than on the basis of race or color" (110 *Cong. Rec.* 13080 [1964]).

2. See the Civil Rights Act of 1964, 42 U.S.C., sec. 2000e-2(e). In particular, Section 703(e) allows for discrimination on the basis of sex, religion, or national origin where such an attribute is "a bona fide occupational qualification that is reasonably necessary to the normal operation of that particular business." This exception to the general antidiscrimination rule has been interpreted very narrowly and does not cover the race preferences of a clientele.

3. See 29 C.F.R., sec. 1604.2 (1989).

4. Federal courts have held that under the business necessity doctrine, expense to the employer is not a permissible reason for discriminating against actual or prospective employees. See *Chrapliwy v. Uniroyal, Inc.*, 485 F. Supp. 252, 271 (1977), citing *Johnson v. Pike Corp. of America*, 332 F. Supp. 490, 495 (1971). They have also held that greater exposure to tort liability from women employees and their offspring does not support a BFOQ exception. See *International Union, UAW v. John Controls*, 111 S. Ct. 1196 (1991). This case also supports the above claim about the employer's concern for the safety of fetuses and future persons not being a BFOQ. The point about customer privacy can be seen in a case where the court did not grant an employer a BFOQ exception where the privacy concerns of clients of a residential retirement home can be satisfied by sex-specific job assignments. See *Fesel v. Masonic Home*, 447 F. Supp. 1346 (1978).

5. The courts have ruled that customer preference, where it is unrelated to the ability to perform a job, does not justify sex discrimination. See *Gerdom v. Continental Airlines*, 692 F. 2d 602 (9th Cir. 1982). They have also ruled that stereotypic impressions of male and female roles do not qualify sex as a BFOQ, *City of Los Angeles Dep't. of Water v. Manhart*, 98 S. Ct. 1370, 1374 (1978), nor do stereotyped customer preferences, *Diaz v. Pan American World Airways, Inc.*, 442 F. 2d 385, 389 (5th Cir. 1971), *cert. den.*, 92 S. Ct. 275, 230 (1971). A valid BFOQ exception cannot rest on the need to accommodate the sexually discriminatory policies of other countries. See *Fernandez v. Wynn Oil Co.*, 653 F. 2d 1273 (9th Cir. 1982). The Equal Employment Opportunity Commission has held that the only customer preference allowed as a BFOQ is one necessary for the purpose of genuineness or authenticity (e.g., that of an actor). See 29 C.F.R., sec. 1604.2(a)(2) (1972).

6. An example of the interpretation of the BFOQ as incorporating a business necessity element can be seen in *Fernandez v. Wynn Oil Co.*, 653 F. 2d 1273, 1276

(1981), where the Ninth Circuit allowed to stand the federal district court's assertions that "sex discrimination must be compelled by business considerations in order to qualify as a BFOQ," and that customer preferences support a bona fide occupational qualification if "no customer will do business with a member of one sex either because it would destroy the essence of the business or would create serious safety and efficacy problems." See also *Diaz*, 442 F. 2d at 388.

7. See *Diaz*, ibid., at 385–389.

8. Elsewhere, the Ninth Circuit held that weight requirements put forth as part of an airline's attempt to feature attractive female cabin attendants would not count as a BFOQ, because the consumer preferences that the airline sought to address were unrelated to the ability to perform the job. See *Gerdom*, 692 F. 2d at 609.

9. See *PGA Tour, Inc. v. Martin*, no. 0024 (2001). The ADA is found at 42 U.S.C., 12101 *et seq.*

10. W. B. Gallie argues that a concept is essentially contestable when it has both evaluative and descriptive elements and ordinary usage does not support a single definition. As a result, the best definition (i.e., the best conception) is a function of substantive argument. See W. B. Gallie, "Essentially Contested Concepts," *Proceedings of the Aristotelian Society* 56 (1956): 167–68. The distinction between concept and conception can also be found in Ronald Dworkin, *Taking Rights Seriously* (Cambridge: Harvard University Press, 1977), 134–35.

11. John Rawls classifies effort-making ability along with other capacities as natural assets and then argues that they are undeserved. See John Rawls, *A Theory of Justice* (Cambridge: Belknap Press of Harvard University, 1971), 103–4, 310–15.

12. This idea can be seen in Bernard Williams, "The Idea of Equality," in *Moral Concepts*, ed. Joel Feinberg (New York: Oxford University Press, 1970), 163–64.

13. This idea can be found in Michael Walzer, *Spheres of Justice* (New York: Basic Books, 1983), 88n.

14. The criticisms in this paragraph all come from Robert Nozick, *Anarchy, State, and Utopia* (New York: Basic Books, 1974), 232–35.

15. Ibid., 234.

16. This notion can be seen in Thomas Nagel, *The View from Nowhere* (New York: Oxford University Press, 1986), 164–88. The other type of reason Nagel brings up is a deontological one, which is an agent-relative reason not to maltreat others in certain ways. Despite the confusing labels, both types of reason might be thought to rest on the value of autonomy, which is a person's shaping himself through the selection of his beliefs and desires.

17. The idea for this point comes from Richard Epstein, *Forbidden Grounds* (Cambridge: Harvard University Press, 1992), 302.

18. Here I do not mean to be committing myself to a fine-grained account of actions where each instantiation of a property constitutes a different act. Rather, my

account is compatible with a coarse-grained account where one action instantiates many properties. The former account can be found in Alvin Goldman, *A Theory of Human Action* (Englewood Cliffs: Prentice Hall, 1970), 20–44, the latter in Donald Davidson, "Actions, Reasons, and Causes," *Journal of Philosophy* 60 (1963): 685–700, and "The Logical Form of Action Sentences," in *The Logic of Decision and Action,* ed. Nicholas Rescher (Pittsburgh: University of Pittsburgh Press, 1967), 81–95.

19. Richard Epstein puts forth a view that is similar to mine. He argues that merit is that to which the employer or employee contracts. See Epstein, *Forbidden Grounds,* 413–14. His argument rests on the idea that there is nothing that an external observer can rely on when assessing merit other than the conditions for market exchange. Instead, there is only the subjective test of desire manifested in consent. There are some significant differences between our theories. First, on his account, merit is a function of the terms of employment, usually the contractual terms. On my account, the employer's preferences determine the qualifications for employment; the contractual terms merely limit the extent to which an employee is obligated to fulfill them. Second, the employee in part determines what constitutes merit. However, on my account, this is not the case, since it is the employer via his ownership of the business that determines the tasks that constitute a job. Third, Epstein's economic justification of a job qualification sharply differs from my nonconsequentialist one. Fourth, Epstein's concern about external observers may involve incorporating epistemic elements into the conception of merit, whereas my account does not. Fifth, Epstein's account does not distinguish the desires that determine work-related merit from other desires, in part because he does not limit it to contexts involving capacities or potentialities, and a willingness to exercise or develop them.

20. A developed autonomy-based defense of property rights can be found in Loren Lomasky, *Persons, Rights, and the Moral Community* (New York: Oxford, 1987), chap. 2–6.

21. I owe this objection to Neil Feit.

22. I owe this objection to Michael Levin.

23. In the economic context, see Norman Daniels, "Meritocracy," in *Justice and Economic Distribution,* 2d ed., ed. John Arthur and William Shaw (Englewood Cliffs: Prentice Hall, 1991), 154–67. In the context of affirmative action, a merit-based argument against affirmative action is provided by Louis P. Pojman, "The Moral Status of Affirmative Action," in *Morality in Practice,* 5th ed., ed. James Sterba (Belmont: Wadsworth, 1997), 238–54, esp. 251. For desert-based arguments that relate to merit, see James Rachels, "What People Deserve," in *Justice and Economic Distribution,* 2d ed., ed. John Arthur and William Shaw (Englewood Cliffs: Prentice Hall, 1991), 154–67 and Stephen Kershnar, "Strong Affirmative Action Programs at State Educational Institutions Cannot Be Justified via Compensatory Justice," *Public Affairs Quarterly* 11 (1997): 345–64.

24. For example, the United States Supreme Court, in *Price Waterhouse v. Hopkins,* 490 U.S. 228, 243, noted that when an employer ignored the attributes enumerated in Title VII of the 1964 Civil Rights Act, Congress hoped it would focus on the qualifications of the applicant or the employee.

25. Charles Lawrence argues that discrimination against blacks in part reflects forces that we are unconscious of rather than the sort of conscious trade-off mentioned earlier. See Charles Lawrence, "The Id, the Ego, and Equal Protection: Reckoning with Unconscious Racism," *Stanford Law Review* 39 (1992): 322–23. Such failures may indicate a lesser degree of autonomy or dignity, but they do not constitute a serious affront to them.

26. The issue here is whether the implicit promise in the offer is a promise to hire the most qualified, a promise to hire the applicant with the greatest propensity to satisfy the employer's preferences, or a promise to do both things. As an empirical matter, the notion that it is a promise to hire in accordance with the second conception alone is false, since this is not a widely held conception of a job qualification. Whether the speech act commits the employer to hire the applicant who is the most qualified on the best understanding of this phrase depends on whether the contractual terms are referentially transparent (i.e., substitution for a co-referential term preserves the sentence's truth-value), or referentially opaque (i.e., not referentially transparent). If instead the term is referentially transparent, then if uptake (i.e., receipt and acceptance) of the promise is present, there may be a promise-based duty to hire the most qualified.

27. In the context of punishment, a wrongdoer's desert does seem to ground a duty in another to impose punishment upon him. However, this can be accounted for via reflexive duties, an account that is not available in the economic context. Stephen Kershnar provides such an account in "Reflexive Retributive Duties," *Jahrbuch fur Recht und Ethik* 8 (2000): 1–14.

28. See George Sher, Qualifications, Fairness, and Desert," in *Equal Opportunity*, ed. Norman Bowie (Boulder: Westview, 1988), 113–27, esp. 123–24. This argument is also found in George Sher, *Desert* (Princeton: Princeton University Press, 1987), 125–31. Sher also argues that merit-based hiring affirms the applicants' involvement in the wider life of the community (ibid., 119–20). I shall not treat this as a separate reason, since it rests on the value of taking the applicants' agency seriously.

29. An interesting discussion of the consequentialist and social-justice arguments for taking into account only some of the employer's preferences is found in Alan Wertheimer, "Jobs, Qualifications, and Preferences," *Ethics* 94 (1983): 99–112, esp. 109–12.

30. I owe this point to Louis P. Pojman.

31. It is worth noting that where preferential treatment for black and Puerto Rican attorneys has become a standard feature of hiring and advancement in a field, such refusal on behalf of clients is not obviously irrational. This is because the lowered standards probably result in such employees being, on average, of lesser ability than those hired and advanced via the standard screening processes.

32. Since students have the second-order capacity to develop the first-order capacities that characterize different types of knowledge, a qualification for an educational institution is usually going to be concerned with a capacity rather than a potentiality.

33. In general, the dropout rate for blacks in the 80s has been twice that of whites. See Herrnstein and Murray, *The Bell Curve* 473, citing the National Center for Education Statistics, *The Condition of Education* (Washington, D.C.: Government Printing Office, 1992), tables 170, 249. At 300 major colleges and universities, among the full-time students who enrolled in degree programs as freshman between 1984 and 1987, only 34 percent of blacks completed a degree within six years versus 57 percent of whites. See Stephan Thernstrom and Abigail Thernstrom, *America in Black and White* (New York: Simon & Schuster, 1999), citing *Journal of Blacks in Higher Education* 5 (Autumn 1994): 44–46. There was an improvement (40 percent degree completion rate) for black freshmen who began college in the 1989–90 year (ibid., citing National Collegiate Athletic Association, *1996 NCAA Division I Graduation-Rates Report* (Overland Park, Kansas, 1996), 622. For persons who started college in the 1992–93 academic year, the dropout rate for blacks at elite colleges was more than twice that of whites and almost three times more at some of them (e.g., Pennsylvania, Duke, Dartmouth, and Stanford) (ibid., at 408, citing Theodore Cross, "What if There Was No Affirmative Action in College Admissions? A Further Refinement of Our Earlier Calculations," *Journal of Blacks in Higher Education* 5 (Autumn 1994): 55.

For freshmen in 1976 and 1989 at a cross section of elite schools, blacks who graduated had significantly lower grades than whites (23rd vs. 53rd percentile). This pattern diminishes but is still present even when we control for SAT scores, high school grades, socioeconomic status, and other factors (e.g., gender, school selectivity, field of student, being an athlete or not). See William G. Bowen and Derek Bok, *The Shape of the River* (Princeton: Princeton University Press, 1998), 72, 77. However, whether the problem is one of a fit between the affirmative-action beneficiaries and their classmates is a fairly complex one, since different results occur if we look at dropout rates than if we look at grades (ibid., 61–64, 82 n. 35).

Some particular examples here are worth noting. For example, at M.I.T. in the mid-1980s, nearly one-fourth of black students failed to graduate, and those that did had lower grades than their classmates. See A. Hu, "Minorities Need More Support," *The Tech*, March 17, 1987, p. 1. At the University of Texas at Austin during the time at which strong affirmative-action programs were still in place, the graduation rate of black students was half that of white students. See Sowell, *Inside American Education*, 145, citing Steven Mays, "Racism in University Admissions," *Texas Review* (March 1989): 6. At the University of California at Berkeley in the 1980s, more than 70 percent of black students failed to graduate. See John Bunzel, "Affirmative Action Admissions: How It 'Works' at Berkeley," *The Public Interest* (Fall 1988): 124–25. This is not surprising, since black SAT scores are considerably lower than white scores at these schools, and the SAT in general slightly overestimates black performance. See Crouse and Trusheim, *The Case against the SAT*, 96–98. This difference in admissions produces lower grades in graduate and professional schools and produces a disproportionately high bar failure rate for blacks. For this last point, see Sowell, *Inside American Education*, 140, citing Salim Muswakkil, "Bias in the Bar Exam?" *Student Lawyer* (January 1980): 14ff.; Sarai Ribicoff, "California's New Bar Exam Tests Charges of Racial Bias," *American Lawyer* (June 1980): 11–12; "Council Will Study Bar Exam Pass Rates to Gauge Bias," *Bar Leader* (May–June 1991): 7–21. It should be noted that these cited authors charge that the test is culturally biased.

34. The mission statements are ambiguous as to the importance attached to diversity and equal opportunity. Some of the mission statements mention the "appreciation of human diversity" (Wayne State University), "campus environment hospitable to multicultural interests" (Brooklyn College), and the value of helping students "learn about . . . their cultural and social heritage" (San Diego State University). However, to the extent that the colleges and university list an overarching interest, it is knowledge and the beneficial effects that come from it. For example, the University of Michigan states that its mission is "to serve the people of Michigan and the world through preeminence in creating, communicating, preserving, and applying knowledge, art, and academic values." Brooklyn College states that "[t]he overarching goal of the educational experience at Brooklyn College is to provide students with the knowledge and skills to live in a globally interdependent world and the support services to help them succeed."

Chapter 2. Strong Affirmative-Action Programs at State Institutions

1. See Alan H. Goldman, "Affirmative Action," in *Equality and Preferential Treatment,* ed. Marshall Cohen et al. (Princeton: Princeton University Press, 1977), 192.

2. It is a mistake to think that all qualifications are earned. For example, the height of certain professional basketball centers is a qualification, insofar as it is an attribute that in general improves one's performance. However, a person is not responsible for and hence does not deserve to be a certain height.

3. The consent account of state authority can be found in Thomas Hobbes and John Locke and has a more recent expression in Robert Nozick, *Anarchy, State, and Utopia* (New York: Basic Books, 1974), chap. 1–6. The duty of fair play is found in H. L. A. Hart, "Are There Any Natural Rights?," in *Theories of Rights,* ed. Jeremy Waldron (New York: Oxford University Press, 1984), 85–86; John Rawls, "The Justification of Civil Disobedience," in *The Duty to Obey the Law,* ed. William Edmundson (Lanham: Rowman & Littlefield, 1999), 49–63; John Rawls, "Legal Obligation and the Duty of Fair Play," in *Law and Philosophy,* ed. Sidney Hook (New York: New York University Press, 1964), 3–18.

4. See Derek Parfit, *Reasons and Persons* (Oxford: Oxford University Press, 1984), 493–502.

5. This type of interest may involve a person receiving treatment that is morally required by a legitimate positive desert claim or by a moral right. Technically, interests include desert, however since the latter has a distinctive type of ground, it is useful to separate them.

6. See J. L. Cowan, "Inverse Discrimination," in *The Affirmative Action Debate,* ed. Steven M. Cahn (New York: Routledge, 1995), 5.

7. I owe this point to a personal conversation with Larry Powers. This objection can also be found in James Rachels, "What People Deserve," in *Justice and Economic*

Distribution, 2d ed., ed. John Arthur and William Shaw (Englewood Cliffs: Prentice Hall, 1991), 147.

8. See Jeffrie Murphy and Jules Coleman, *Philosophy of Law,* 2d ed. (Boulder: Westview Press, 1990), 159.

9. I leave aside the issue of whether there is a single relevantly similar possible world or an infinite sequence of them. Also, because there might be such an infinite sequence, I have chosen to focus on the relevantly similar rather than the nearest possible world.

10. This example comes from Lawrence Lombard.

11. This view fits nicely with, but is not entailed by, Alvin Goldman's definition of an act token as the exemplifying of an act property by the agent at a particular time (and possibly in a particular manner). See Goldman, *A Theory of Human Action,* 10. It also relates to the idea that an event's cause is an essential feature of it. See Peter van Inwagen, "Ability and Responsibility," *Philosophical Review* 87 (1978): 201–24. On this view, the properly structured counterfactual is an epistemic guide, but not the actual criterion for a token harm.

12. See James Sterba, "Justice and the Concept of Desert," *The Personalist* (1976): 195.

13. See George Sher, "Compensation and Transworld Personal Identity," *The Monist* 62 (1979): 378–391.

14. George Sher, "Ancient Wrongs and Modern Rights," *Philosophy and Public Affairs* 10 (1980): 3–17. Also see George Sher, "Justifying Reverse Discrimination in Employment," in *Equality and Preferential Treatment,* ed. Marshall Cohen et al. (Princeton: Princeton University Press, 1977), 55–57.

15. See D'Souza, *The End of Racism,* 113.

16. See Robert Fullinwider, "Preferential Hiring and Compensation," in *The Affirmative Action Debate,* ed. Steven Cahn (New York: Routledge, 1995), 87–88.

17. Ibid.

18. In the context of punishment, this justification has been put forth as a justification for failing to respect other duties owed to persons. See Alan H. Goldman, "The Paradox of Punishment," in *Punishment,* ed. A. John Simmons et al. (Princeton: Princeton University Press, 1995), 31.

19. The idea for these conditions comes from Michael S. Moore, "The Moral and Metaphysical Sources of Criminal Law," in *Criminal Justice: Nomos XXVII,* ed. J. R. Pennock and J. W. Chapman (New York: New York University, 1985), 13–14.

20. I am using the phrase "intentional act" to refer to an act that is done purposely, knowingly, or recklessly. Robert Audi has pointed out to me that contrary to parts of the American criminal law, I am assuming that a negligent state of mind is not sufficient for moral guilt. This assumption, however, is not crucial, since a convincing argument can be made that many white males are not negligent with regard to their choice of political activities.

21. See Jules Coleman, "Corrective Justice and Wrongful Gain," in *Philosophy of Law,* 4th ed., ed. Joel Feinberg and Hyman Gross (Belmont: Wadsworth, 1991), 429–30.

22. This example comes from Joel Feinberg, "Voluntary Euthanasia and the Right to Life," *Philosophy and Public Affairs* 7 (1978): 93.

23. For the purpose of this analysis, we need not address whether every unjust act involves a right infringement.

24. In addition, there is a problem with the interaction of relevant counterfactuals. For example, the ancestors of many young white males, such as those who descend from twentieth-century Irish and Jewish immigrants, may themselves have faced unjust discrimination, thereby producing a multigenerational competitive disadvantage that reduces the relative disadvantage that black students suffer as a result of past discrimination. Such effects ought to be balanced against one another, which will turn out to be a difficult task.

25. Some important cases in the tort law appear to conflict with the causation requirement. For example, in *Summers v. Tice,* 199 P. 2d 1 (1948), the court held that two defendants who were negligent in shooting their shotguns at the plaintiff were jointly and severally liable for the plaintiff's injuries, even though only one of them caused each of the injuries. In *Sindell v. Abbott Laboratories,* 607 P. 2d 924 (Cal. 1980), the court faced a products liability case where the plaintiff could not identify which defendant-manufacturers produced the allegedly harm-inducing drug. The court held that the defendant-manufacturers were liable for a percentage of the injury, where this percentage was equal to the market-share percentage of the drug that each defendant produced. I think that even if such cases were correctly decided, and I doubt that they were, they are better understood as evidentiary rulings rather than a denial of the causation requirement. They, in effect, transferred the burden of evidence from the plaintiff to the defendants, a transfer that may be justified by fairness (i.e., ensuring that the burden lies on the negligent parties rather than on the innocent victim) or efficiency (i.e., shifting the burden of injury onto those who will take the most efficient precautions). My interpretation is supported by the opportunity of each defendant in these and many subsequent cases to show that it did not cause the injury.

26. The latter view is set out in Richard Posner, "The Concept of Corrective Justice in Recent Theories of Tort Law," in *Philosophy of Law* 4th ed., ed. Joel Feinberg and Hyman Gross (Belmont: Wadsworth, 1991), 417–28.

27. This type of approach, absent reference to American law, is found in Bernard R. Boxill, "The Morality of Reparations," in *The Affirmative Action Debate,* ed. Steven M. Cahn (New York: Routledge, 1995), 113.

28. See Judith Jarvis Thomson, "Preferential Hiring," in *Equality and Preferential Treatment,* ed. Marshall Cohen et al. (Princeton: Princeton University Press, 1977), 19–39.

29. Robert Amdur provides a similar principle. See Robert Amdur, "Compensatory Justice: The Question of Costs," in *The Affirmative Action Debate,* ed. Steven M. Cahn (New York: Routledge, 1995), 96.

30. This account of rights can be found in Ronald Dworkin, "Rights As Trumps," in *Theories of Rights,* ed. Jeremy Waldron (New York: Oxford University Press, 1984), 153–67.

31. This view of rights can be found in Nozick, *Anarchy, State, and Utopia,* 26–33. An analogous view of morality can be found in Warren S. Quinn, "Actions, Intentions, and Consequences: The Doctrine of Doing and Allowing," in *Killing and Letting Die,* 2d ed., ed. Bonnie Steinbock and Alastair Norcross (New York: Fordham University Press, 1994), 370–76.

32. Fred Feldman defends justice-adjusted consequentialism in "Adjusting Utility for Justice: A Consequentialist Reply to the Objection from Justice," *Philosophy and Phenomenological Research* 55 (1995): 567–85. Amartya Sen discusses consequentialism's ability to incorporate rights in "Rights and Agency," in *Consequentialism and Its Critics,* ed. Samuel Scheffler (New York: Oxford University Press, 1988), 187–223. Shelly Kagan discusses the relation of well-being to desert in determining the goodness of an outcome in "Equality and Desert," in *What Do We Deserve?,* ed. Louis P. Pojman and Owen McLeod (New York: Oxford University Press, 1999), 298–314.

33. I owe this point to Mark van Roojen.

34. The necessary relation between duties accompanying rights and the ability to waive those duties is defended in H. L. A. Hart, "Are There Any Natural Rights?" in *Theories of Rights,* ed. Jeremy Waldron (New York: Oxford University Press, 1984), 81–82.

Chapter 3. Uncertain Damages to Racial Minorities and Strong Affirmative Action

1. The notion that in almost all, if not all, cases motive does not affect the deontic status of an act and the following example come from Michael Gorr, "Motives and Rightness," *Philosophia* 27 (1999): 588–94. The assertion is also defended by W. D. Ross in *The Right and the Good* (Indianapolis: Hackett, 1988), 4–6. The arguments for this account of rightness rest on the claim that motives are not directly enough controlled by the agent to support an ought statement, that there is conceptual and pragmatic value in being able to distinguish an agent's blameworthiness/praiseworthiness from the status of his or her actions, and that the distinction tracks the way in which we ordinarily use language (e.g., "Joe did the right thing but for all the wrong reasons"). However, it is worth noting that ordinary language at times conflicts with this distinction. In addition, if the motive theorist adopts the view that (1) one's duty is to act from a certain motive and (2) the motive from which we must act is the sense of duty, then a vicious circle results and makes such an account untenable. See Ross, *The Right and the Good,* 5–6.

2. A wrongdoing is an intentional act that violates a person's (significant) moral right and harms (or usually harms) a person. A person is culpable for a wrongdoing if and only if it was done under conditions that make it fair (and truthful) to attribute

the act to the person's decision and will, it was done by a person who has the capacities to be a moral agent, and the attribution to the person is not mitigated by other factors.

3. See Jules Coleman, "On the Moral Argument for the Fault System," *Journal of Philosophy* 71 (1974): 473–90; Jules Coleman, "Corrective Justice and Wrongful Gain," in *Philosophy of Law,* 5th ed., ed. Joel Feinberg and Hyman Gross (Belmont: Wadsworth, 1995), 385–396; Jeffrie Murphy and Jules Coleman, *Philosophy of Law,* 2nd ed. (Boulder: Westview, 1990), 158–61.

4. Coleman, "On the Moral Argument for the Fault System," 489–90.

5. Coleman, "Corrective Justice and Wrongful Gain," 387.

6. This example is mine not Coleman's. The batterer does not gain any political liberty that he would not otherwise have had, since liberty occurs within the framework of moral rights, and the murderer does not gain a moral right, nor does he gain legal or moral permission to violate the legal and moral rights of others.

7. Coleman, "On the Moral Argument for the Fault System," 473–90.

8. Related arguments can be found in Gerald F. Gaus, "Does Compensation Restore Equality?" *Nomos* (33) (1991): 56–60; Richard Posner, "The Concept of Corrective Justice in Recent Theories of Tort Law," *Journal of Legal Studies* 10 (1981): 187–206.

9. George Sher and Judith Jarvis Thomson identify this as an unfair advantage that white males gain as a result of prior unjust acts. See George Sher, "Justifying Reverse Discrimination in Employment," in *The Affirmative Action Debate,* ed. Steven M. Cahn (New York: Routledge, 1995), 73–75; Thomson, "Preferential Hiring," 38–39.

10. Thomas Nagel and George Sher identity this as an unfair advantage that white males gain as a result of prior unjust acts. See Thomas Nagel, "Equal Treatment and Compensatory Discrimination," *Philosophy and Public Affairs* 8 (1973): 360; George Sher, "Preferential Hiring," in *Just Business,* ed. Tom Regan (Philadelphia: Temple University Press, 1983), 48.

11. I leave aside the issue of whether or not causal statements reduce to counterfactual statements.

12. Versions of this argument can be found in D'Souza, *The End of Racism,* 113; Ellen Frankel Paul, "Set-Asides, Reparations, and Compensatory Justice," *Compensatory Justice: Nomos XXXIII* (New York: New York University Press, 1993), 119.

13. The underlying assumption here is that the identity of one's parents is an essential property of a person. On some accounts, this follows from the more general principle that the origin of an object is essential to it. See Saul Kripke, "Naming and Necessity," in *Semantics of Natural Language,* 2d ed., ed. Donald Davidson and Gilbert Harman (Boston: D. Reidel, 1972), 351, n. 57. These accounts probably depend on a physicalist account of personal identity. The idea for this point comes from Geoffrey Madell, *The Identity of the Self* (Edinburgh: The University Press, 1981), 80–87.

14. This argument can be seen in Michael E. Levin, "Reverse Discrimination, Shackled Runners, and Personal Identity," *Philosophical Studies* 37 (1980): 143; Ellen Frankel Paul, "Set-Asides, Reparations, and Compensatory Justice," *Compensatory Justice: Nomos XXXIII*, ed. John Chapman (New York: New York University Press, 1993), 119; Onora O'Neill, "Rights to Compensation," *Social Philosophy and Policy* 5 (1987): 81; Samuel C. Wheeler, "Reparations Reconstructed," *American Philosophical Quarterly* 34 (1997): 302–3. George Sher also brings up this argument, although he does so in a different context. See George Sher "Compensation and Transworld Personal Identity," *The Monist* 62 (1979): 388–90.

15. The idea for this point comes from Lawrence Powers.

16. There are exceptions to this rule, such as crimes of possession and cases in which the defendant causes the victim to be in danger and then omits to act, but these cases might be properly viewed as involving complex commissions of which one element is an omission.

17. Restatement 2d of Torts, Sec. 314.

18. For example, a recent case involving the University of Texas Law School found that, on average, admitted Mexican-American students had noticeably lower grade point averages and standardized test scores than admitted white students. See *Hopwood v. State of Tex.*, 78 F. 2d 932, 936–38 (5th Cir. 1996).

19. Two general types of evidence support the notion that IQ is genetically inherited. See Herrnstein and Murray, *The Bell Curve*, 105–8. One type of evidence involves samples of blood relatives, especially identical twins who were raised apart. These studies allow us to compare the IQs of persons with shared genes who were raised in different environments. The second type of evidence involves samples of persons with different levels of shared genes raised in similar environments. Some studies use both types of evidence. Herrnstein and Murray assert that the results of the hundreds of studies on this topic support the claim that about 40 percent to 80 percent of a person's IQ is genetically inherited (ibid., 105).

20. Herrnstein and Murray, *The Bell Curve*, 275, citing M. Storfer, *Intelligence and Giftedness* (San Francisco: Jossey Bass, 1990) and Richard Lynn, "Intelligence: Ethnicity and Culture," in *Cultural Diversity and the Schools*, ed. J. Lynch and C. Modgil (London: Falmer Press, 1992), 361–87. See also Richard Lynn, "Intelligence, Income, and Ethnic Identity in the United States," *Public Interest* 20 (1995): 347, citing K. MacDonald, *A People that Shall Dwell Alone* (Westport: Praeger, 1994), and Storfer, *Intelligence and Giftedness*.

21. Richard Lynn, "Recent Data on Racial and Ethnic Differences in Intelligence in the United States," *Personality and Individual Differences* (1996): 271–73; Richard Lynn, "The Intelligence of the Mongoloids: A Psychometric, Evolution, and Neurological Theory," *Personality and Individual Differences* 8 (1987): 813–26.

22. Thomas Sowell, *Civil Rights: Rhetoric or Reality?* (New York: Quill, 1984), 43–46. For example, persons of German descent have been successful in craftsmanship, technology, and science in a number of countries. See Thomas Sowell, *Ethnic America*

(New York: Basic Books, 1981), 52–53, 58–59. In many countries, the Chinese have been disproportionately represented in technical fields such as mathematics, science, and technology. See Sowell, *Civil Rights: Rhetoric or Reality?*, 27–28.

23. See Meredith Bagby, *Annual Report of the United States of America* (New York: McGraw-Hill, 1997), 5, citing the U.S. Census Bureau, 1994. See also U.S. Dept. of Health and Human Services, *Vital Statistics of the United States,* vol. 1 (Washington, D.C.: Government Printing Office, 1991).

24. See Neil Alan Weiner and Marvin E. Wolfgang, "The Extent and Character of Violent Crime in America, 1969 to 1982," in *Violence,* ed. Neil Alan Weiner et al. (Harcourt Brace Jovanovich, 1990), 32.

25. See J. Philippe Rushton, "Race Differences in Behavior: A Review and Evolutionary Analysis," *Personality and Individual Differences* 9 (1988): 1016; Michael J. Hindelang, "Race and Involvement in Common Personal Crime, *American Sociological Review* 4 (1978): 100–1.

26. See Charles Murray, "Affirmative Racism," in *Social Ethics,* 4th ed., ed. Thomas A. Mappes and Jane S. Zembaty (New York: McGraw-Hill, 1992), 325–33. Race-based conclusions about persons may even be rational in cases where we lack adequate individualized information about those persons. Michael Levin argues for this conclusion in the context of crime. See Michael Levin, "Responses to Race Differences in Crime," *Journal of Social Philosophy* 23 (1992): 5–29; Michael Levin, "Reply to Adler, Cox, and Corlett," *Journal of Social Philosophy* 25 (1994): 5–19.

27. See D'Souza, *The End of Racism,* 325.

28. See Sowell, *Inside American Education,* 141–48.

29. Robert Simon, "Preferential Hiring: A Reply to Judith Jarvis Thomson," in *Equality and Preferential Treatment,* ed. Marshall Cohen et al. (Princeton: Princeton University Press, 1977), 47.

CHAPTER 4. THE INHERITANCE-BASED CLAIM TO REPARATIONS

1. See Randall Robinson, *The Debt: What America Owes to Blacks* (New York: Dutton, 2000).

2. CBS News, "Reparations for Slavery," cbs.kgan.com (2000), p. 1.

3. Larry Neal and James Marketti estimate that the value of unpaid income to slaves amounts to $1.4 and $3.4 trillion, respectively. See D'Souza, *The End of Racism,* p. 69, n. 18, citing Richard F. America, ed., *The Wealth of Races: The Present Value of Benefits from Past Injustices* (New York: Greenwood Press, 1990). Richard America estimates that the United States owes black Americans $5 to $10 trillion for slavery. See James Harper, "About Reparations: Bethune Puts the Issue On Trial," *www. blackvoices.com* (2001), p. 1.

4. This argument can be seen in Christopher W. Morris, "Existential Limits to the Rectification of Past Wrongs," *American Philosophical Quarterly* 21 (1984): 175–82; Michael E. Levin, "Reverse Discrimination, Shackled Runners, and Personal Identity," *Philosophical Studies* 37 (1980): 143; Ellen Frankel Paul, "Set-Asides, Reparations, and Compensatory Justice," *Nomos* 33 (1991): 119; Onora O'Neill, "Rights to Compensation," *Social Philosophy and Policy* 5 (1987): 81. George Sher also brings up this argument, although he does so in a different context. See George Sher, "Compensation and Transworld Personal Identity," *The Monist* 62 (1979): 388–90.

5. Versions of this argument can be found in D'Souza, *The End of Racism,* p. 113, and in Paul, "Set-Asides, Reparations, and Compensatory Justice," 119.

6. My assumption here is that the notion of proximate cause cannot by itself ground the relevant intuition.

7. See Joel Feinberg, *Harm to Others* (New York: Oxford University Press, 1984), 95–104.

8. Ibid.

9. This idea comes from David Benatar, "Why It Is Better Never to Come into Existence," *American Philosophical Quarterly* 34 (1997): 345.

10. The idea for this objection comes from Michael Tonderum.

11. I leave aside the issue of whether or not causal statements reduce to counterfactual statements.

12. This model can be seen in Feinberg, *Harm to Others,* 53–54.

13. Derek Parfit argues that causing a person to exist does *benefit* her, even though it does not make her position any *better*. See Derek Parfit, *Reasons and Persons* (Oxford: Clarendon Press, 1984), 487–90. This account rests on a broader view of benefits and harms than the one I invoke above, but if successful, it can account for the gratitude in question.

14. I owe this objection to Neil Feit.

15. This idea comes from Larry Lombard.

16. This point comes from Seana Valentine Shiffrin, "Wrongful Life, Procreative Responsibility, and the Significance of Harm," *Legal Theory* 5 (1999): 122.

17. A third counterintuitive result of this model is that it suggests that there is no morally significant difference between equivalent failures to prevent harm and provide a benefit, since both can be measured in terms of a similarly sized deviation from a counterfactual baseline (ibid., 127–31). This is problematic in that it intuitively seems much worse to harm someone than to refuse to benefit her. The intuitive notion can be accounted in part by the fact that the imposition of harm but not the failure to provide a benefit often involves a right infringement. It can also be accounted for in part by the fact that the imposition of harm usually reflects a worse moral character than the failure to provide a benefit.

18. Note that the point at which the last generation of slaves reproduced need not be the moment at which a person comes into existence, since on many accounts a being does not become a person at conception. I leave aside discussion of the idea that reproduction occurs when the slave's progeny becomes a person rather than at conception.

19. Recent case law seems to sharply restrict the ability of children to recover for harm to their parents. *Ferriter v. Daniel O'Connell's Sons, Inc.*, 413 N.E. 2d 690 (Mass. 1980), held that children may recover for loss of society and companionship as a result of injuries done to their parent, but only if the children are minors who are dependent on the parent for nurture and development. Similar results occur in *Berger v. Weber*, 303 N.W. 2d 424 (1981) and in *Weitl v. Moes*, 311 N.W. 2d 259 (Iowa 1981). It is not clear whether recovery under this line of cases requires that the children exist at the time the injury occurred, although such restrictions might in any case reflect pragmatic concerns.

20. Thomas Nagel and George Sher identify this as an unfair advantage that white males gain as a result of prior unjust acts. See Thomas Nagel, "Equal Treatment and Compensatory Discrimination," *Philosophy and Public Affairs* 8 (1973): 360; George Sher, "Preferential Hiring," in *Just Business*, ed. Tom Regan (Philadelphia: Temple University Press, 1983), 48.

21. The idea for this objection comes from Lawrence Powers.

22. The idea for the constructive trust model comes from George Schedler.

23. *Black's Law Dictionary*, 5th ed., s.v. "Constructive trust."

24. Feinberg, *Harm to Others*, 79–95.

25. On some accounts, promises are a type of conventional speech act that has illocutionary force. See John Searle, "What Is a Speech Act?" in *Philosophy of Language*, 2d ed., ed. A. P. Martinich (New York: Oxford University Press, 1990), 120–25; John Searle, "How to Derive 'Ought' from 'Is'," in *Theories of Ethics*, ed. Philippa Foot (New York: Oxford University Press, 1990), 101–14. On such an account, they may be independent of institutions (bodies that have authority over others), even if they are dependent of conventions. The notion that contracts and gifts are types of promises is defended in Charles Fried, *Contract As Promise* (Cambridge: Harvard University Press, 1981).

26. See Bernard R. Boxill, *Blacks and Social Justice*, 2d ed. (Lanham: Rowman & Littlefield, 1992), 153–54. Michael D. Bayles discusses the idea that reparations are owed to groups and not to individuals, but he does not clearly endorse the idea. See Michael D. Bayles, "Reparations to Wronged Groups," in *The Affirmative Action Debate*, ed. Steven M. Cahn (New York: Routledge, 1995), 15–18.

27. This is not to say that current membership is an essential condition of a group. Instead, the group's claims might be parasitic on the claims of whatever persons stand in certain relations with either the proper causal-historical links to the collection that founded the group and the relations that also in part constituted the original group or was in an ancestral relation to this collection and relations. This approach suggests but does not obviously commit me to the notion that the initial membership and relations binding these group members are essential conditions of it.

28. Some of the ideas for this argument come from George Sher, "Preferential Hiring," in *Just Business,* ed. Tom Regan (Philadelphia: Temple University Press, 1983), 36–37, and Michael Tooley, "Abortion and Infanticide," in *The Rights and Wrongs of Abortion,* ed. Marshall Cohen et al. (Princeton: Princeton University Press, 1974), 58–65.

29. George Schedler objects that compensation for slavery is not owed for coerced labor, on the basis that the relevant baseline is a world in which the work is not done or done by other workers. See George Schedler, *Racist Symbols and Reparations* (Lanham: Rowman & Littlefield, 1998), 101, 107–9. Still, in the world in which slavery occurs, the slave's interest in receiving just compensation for her work is set back.

30. The other things being equal condition screens out a range of irrelevant variables (e.g., irrational preferences and evidentiary problems).

31. David Friedman, "What Is 'Fair Compensation' for Death or Injury?" *International Review of Law and Economics* 2 (1982): 85.

32. Other adjustments would also have to be made. For example, there may be a diminishing marginal utility for injured parties that ought not be factored into the compensation that is owed. Friedman, "What Is 'Fair Compensation' for Death or Injury?," 82–83.

Chapter 5. Reject the Inheritance-Based Claim to Reparations

1. Herrnstein and Murray argue for the existence of such differences in *The Bell Curve,* ch. 13. Their argument has received a lot of criticism. For example, some authors have argued that racial mistreatment and not genetics may account for the data that are used to support the notion of high intraracial heritability of IQ. See Ned Block, "How Heritability Misleads about Race," *Cognition* 56 (1995): 99–128; C. Jencks, *Rethinking Social Policy* (Cambridge: Harvard University Press, 1991), 99, 107; Andrew Hacker, *Two Nations* (New York: Scribner's, 1992), 27. Others object that the inference from genotype to phenotype with a particular IQ that underlies the finding of interracial genetic differences in intelligence is flawed, because the phenotypical patterns may change when we consider unobserved environments. See Block, "How Heritability Misleads about Race," figures 4 and 5, D. Layzer,"Science or Superstitution: A Physical Scientist Looks at the IQ Controversy," in *The IQ Controversy,* ed. N. Block and G. Dworkin (New York: Pantheon, 1976), 194–241. There are also general objections to the inference from IQ test scores to different genetic aptitudes. Among the more general objections are that there is no such thing as intelligence (as opposed to multiple distinct abilities), and even if there is such a thing as intelligence it is not measured by IQ tests, and in any case, environmental factors alone explain intragroup, and intergroup differences. The summary of the different objections, along with a critical response to them, occurs in Michael Levin, *Why Race Matters* (Westport: Praeger, 1997), ch. 3–4, and Max Hocutt and Michael Levin, "The *Bell Curve* Case for Heredity," *Philosophy of the Social Sciences* 29 (1999): 389–415.

2. An extended defense of this claim is provided in Sowell, *Civil Rights: Rhetoric or Reality?* (New York: Quill, 1984), ch. 1.

3. I owe this objection to an anonymous reviewer.

4. Studies of identical twins raised in different families have a high degree of similarity in intelligence. This suggests that intelligence is, to a significant degree, heritable. These studies are summarized in T. J. Bouchard, "The Genetic Architecture of Human Intelligence," in *Biological Approaches to the Study of Human Intelligence,* ed. P. A. Vernon (Norwood, N.J.: Ablex, 1993). Adoption studies where black children have IQ test scores closer to their genetic parents than their adopted white parents suggests that the interracial difference in intelligence is genetic. See R. Weinberg, S. Scarr, and I. Waldman, "The Minnesota Transracial Adoption Study: A Follow-up of IQ Test Performance at Adolescence," *Intelligence* 16 (1992): 117–35. Herrnstein and Murray estimate that the black-white difference in intelligence is significant (one standard deviation) and that roughly 60 percent of it is hereditary. See Herrnstein and Murray, *The Bell Curve,* 276–80, 298–99.

5. See Herrnstein and Murray, *The Bell Curve,* ch. 5–12.

6. For example, an efficiency-based defense of property rights can be found in Harold Demsetz, "Toward a Theory of Property Rights," *American Economic Review: Proceedings and Papers* 57 (1967): 347–59. A desert-based defense of income earned via sacrifice can be found in Joel Feinberg, *Doing and Deserving* (Princeton: Princeton University Press, 1970), 88–94, and a general defense of desert to the object of one's hard work can be found in George Sher, *Desert* (Princeton: Princeton University Press, 1987), ch. 4.

7. Here I am not committing myself to the stronger claim that compensatory justice allows a debt of compensation to be discharged by a person other than the one that caused the harm. Such a view is defended in Jules Coleman, "Corrective Justice and Wrongful Gain," *Journal of Legal Studies* 11 (1982): 421–40.

8. This point invalidates an argument from George Schedler. He argues that since slave owners did not receive any ill-gotten gains (at least by the end of the Civil War), they do not owe any compensation on these grounds. See Schedler, *Racist Symbols and Reparations,* 114–15. However, given the above point, it can be seen that whether they benefited is irrelevant to the issue of whether they owe damages for the token harm that they have caused.

9. See Michael Levin, "Responses to Race Differences in Crime," *Journal of Social Philosophy* 23 (1991): 5, citing "The Black-on-Black Crime Plague," *U.S. News and World Report* (August 22, 1988): 54.

10. See Michael Levin, *Why Race Matters* (Westport: Praeger, 1997), 259. I suspect that Levin underestimates the degree of the transfer, since he underestimates the progressivity of the income tax, but I will leave aside such an argument as it is irrelevant in this context.

11. The fugitive slave laws refer to federal laws passed in 1793 and 1850 and to the Constitution, Art. IV, Sec. 2. The 1793 law, for example, permitted slave owners

and their agents to apprehend fugitives in any state or territory but did not give judges the power to issue arrest warrants or require federal marshals to assist owners. The federal marshals played an active role in the enforcement of these laws. See Michael F. Holt, *The Political Crisis of the 1850s* (New York: Norton, 1978), 89–90.

12. Schedler, *Racist Symbols and Reparations,* 117.

13. The Civil War involved Northern states using aggression to prevent Southern states from withdrawing from the union. This aggression was illegal if the Constitution permitted such unilateral withdrawal, and this depends on the Constitution's language, the ratifying state legislature's intent, and perhaps theories of contractual interpretation. A Southern claim to compensation might also require that the Northern aggression was all-things-considered unjust as well as illegal. I leave these issues aside as they will take us far afield.

14. This account is dependent on a theory of interests and rights. This is common with regard to theories of justice (e.g., retributivism), which also depend on a theory of these elements. Note that the demands of compensatory justice may differ from the tort law and portions of contract law, since the law is often motivated and justified in terms of utilitarian concerns that are probably not a part of justice. For example, it is argued that where the optimal method of accident avoidance is greater care rather than less economic activity, efficiency favors a negligence criterion for liability. See William T. Landes and Richard A. Posner, *The Economic Structure of Tort Law* (Cambridge: Harvard University Press, 1987), ch. 3, esp. p. 70.

15. George Schedler points out that in law, an innocent buyer may sometimes receive legal ownership despite his purchasing tainted goods. For example, where a victim entrusts his goods to a merchant who deals in goods of that type and who sells them to an innocent purchaser, the victim cannot recover the goods against the innocent purchaser. The law holds that the victim has implied that the merchant is the owner or has authority over them. See Steven Emanuel, *Property,* 4th ed. (Larchmont: Emanuel Law Outlines, 1993), 11–12, and the Uniform Commercial Code 2–402, especially section 2. This feature is probably justified by the efficiency gain that occurs by eliminating the incentive for purchasers to investigate the lineage of goods or to buy insurance to cover the risk that the goods are tainted.

16. The idea is discussed in Robert Nozick, *Anarchy, State, and Utopia* (New York: Basic Books, 1974), 152–53, 230–31, and David Lyons, "The New Indian Claims and Original Rights to Land," in *Reading Nozick,* ed. Jeffrey Paul (Totowa, N.J.: Rowman & Littlefield, 1981), 355–79. The situation is more complex, since where the victim and her inheritors and intended beneficiaries are all dead, an account must be given of the status of the good. For example, does it revert to being unowned? Does it become common property?

17. Some consequentialist accounts posit that moral entities such as desert and rights in part determine the goodness of a state of affairs. See, e.g., Fred Feldman, "Adjusting Utility for Justice: A Consequentialist Reply to the Objection from Justice," in *What Do We Deserve?,* ed. Louis P. Pojman and Owen McLeod (New York: Oxford University Press, 1999), 259–70; Amartya Sen, "Rights and Agency," in *Consequential-*

ism and Its Critics, ed. Samuel Scheffler (New York: Oxford University Press, 1988), 187–223. Nothing in principle prevents the consequentialist from including certain principles of (or rights to) compensatory justice into her account.

CHAPTER 6. INTRINSIC MORAL VALUE AND RACIAL DIFFERENCES

1. This type of violation of the categorical imperative is discussed in Allen Wood, "Humanity As an End in Itself," in *Kant's Groundwork of the Metaphysics of Morals,* ed. Paul Guyer (Lanham: Rowman & Littlefield, 1998), 177–84.

2. These two examples come from Thaddeus Metz, "Censure Theory and Intuitions about Punishment," *Law and Philosophy* 19 (2000): 495, 497.

3. In support of the notion that this expression justifies punishment, see, e.g., Metz, "Censure Theory and Intuitions about Punishment," 491–512; Jean Hampton, "An Expressive Theory of Retribution," in *Retributivism and Its Critics,* ed. Wesley Cragg (Stuttgart: F. Steiner Verlag, 1992), 1–25; Igor Primoratz, "Punishment As Language," *Philosophy* 64 (1989): 187–205. The notion that the torture fails to recognize the dignity of criminals and thereby violates the Kantian imperative can be seen in Jeffrie G. Murphy, "Cruel and Unusual Punishments," *Retribution, Justice, and Therapy* (Boston: D. Reidel, 1979), 223–49.

4. Wood cites Proposition 187, a proposed law in California that would have denied non-emergency benefits to illegal aliens, as an example of such contempt. See Wood, "Humanity As End in Itself," 178–80.

5. See Thomas E. Hill Jr., "The Message of Affirmative Action," in *The Affirmative Action Debate,* ed. Steven M. Cahn (New York: Routledge, 1995), 169–72. A similar notion can be found in Ronald Dworkin's analysis of the constitutional right not to be excluded from a state institution on the basis of race. Dworkin analyzes this right in terms of whether it was generated by and signaled contempt. See Ronald Dworkin, "Why Bakke Has No Case," in *Philosophy of Law,* ed. Frederick Schauer and Walter Sinnott-Armstrong (Fort Worth: Harcourt Brace, 1996), 578.

6. Hill, "The Message of Affirmative Action," 189.

7. The notion that the right is independent of motive rests on several claims. First, motives are not directly enough controlled by the agent to support an ought statement. Second, there is conceptual and pragmatic value in being able to distinguish an agent's blameworthiness/praiseworthiness from the status of his actions. Third, this distinction tracks the way in which we ordinarily use language (e.g., "Joe did the right thing but for all the wrong reasons"). However, it is worth noting that ordinary language at times also conflicts with this distinction. Fourth, if the motive theorist adopts the view that (1) one's duty is to act from a certain motive and (2) the motive from which we must act is the sense of duty, then an infinite regress results.

8. Harry Frankfurt's account is found in "Freedom of the Will and the Concept of a Person," in *Free Will,* ed. Gary Watson (New York: Oxford University Press, 1982),

81–95, and "Identification and Wholeheartedness," in *Responsibility, Character, and the Emotions,* ed. Ferdinand Schoeman (New York: Cambridge University Press, 1987), 27–45.

9. First-order desires trivially produce instrumental second-order desires (e.g., the desire to eliminate competitor first-order desires). See Dennis Loughrey, "Second-Order Desire Accounts of Autonomy," *International Journal of Philosophical Studies* 6 (1998): 216–21. I mean to focus on other second-order desires.

10. In fact, there is some evidence in favor of the notion that greater intelligence (one factor of a person's degree of autonomy) correlates with moral behavior. This can be seen in that the more intelligent have a greater tendency to avoid crime, out-of-wedlock births, and welfare usage. For example, chronic criminals have an IQ significantly lower than the average citizen, and a significant part of the tendency of persons of lesser intelligence to perform criminal acts cannot be accounted for by socioeconomic factors. Similarly, out-of-wedlock births are also significantly correlated with a lower level of intelligence, even after the role of socioeconomic status is factored out. With regard to welfare dependency, the picture becomes more complicated, although again intelligence seems to play a role. While the latter two act-types might not be wrong per se, they might be seen as wrong insofar as they carry with them costs that have to be paid by innocent third parties, especially taxpayers. In support of the empirical claims, see Herrnstein and Murray, *The Bell Curve,* ch. 8–10.

11. These two examples come from Joseph Raz, *The Morality of Freedom* (New York: Clarendon Press, 1986), 373–77.

12. A similar coherentist account of autonomy can be found in Laura Waddell Ekstrom, "A Coherence Theory of Autonomy," *Philosophy and Phenomenological Research* 53 (1993): 599–616.

13. This argument can be seen in Gerald Dworkin, *The Theory and Practice of Autonomy* (New York: Cambridge University Press, 1988), 29–31.

14. This distinction can be seen in Joel Feinberg, *Harm to Self* (New York: Oxford University Press, 1986), 27–44.

15. See Feinberg, *Harm to Self,* 33–35.

16. Here I am explicitly rejecting the Kantian notion that autonomy (and autonomous action) must involve self-legislation involving only principles derived from a priori reason. The Kantian account leaves out too much in life that seems important both for morality and for a rich personal life. This point comes from Thomas May, "The Concept of Autonomy," *American Philosophical Quarterly* 31 (1994): 138–39. For example, it seems that I am acting in a way that is both morally right and morally good when at great expense I buy my sister a house out of love for her. In addition, it seems that I do so autonomously if I do so after critical reflection on my self that leads me to conclude that being part of a family is a central part of my identity and that such a role leads to my being bound by certain obligations to family members.

17. The idea for this point comes from Dworkin, *The Theory and Practice of Autonomy,* 15–16.

18. An argument in support of this claim can be seen in Jonathan Glover's argument that mere consciousness cannot account for the greater weight placed on fully functioning adult human beings than on other animals. See his *Causing Death and Saving Lives* (London: Penguin Books, 1977), 48–50.

19. The movies that bring out these intuitions for me are *The Day the Earth Stood Still* (Twentieth Century Fox, 1951), *Alien Nation* (Twentieth Century Fox, 1988), and *Coneheads* (Paramount, 1993).

20. There could even be an inverse correlation between intelligence and autonomy as a condition, however implausible this might be, and it would not endanger my argument. For example, if persons with greater intelligence have more fragile egos, less of a sense of self, or a greater tendency toward rationalizing poor choices, these effects would probably result in such persons having less autonomy as a condition. However, this would not affect my argument, since it focuses on autonomy as a capacity.

21. While some well-known accounts of autonomy assert that autonomy as a capacity is a threshold property not one of degree, they do not provide an argument for this position. The threshold notion of autonomy can be seen in Rawls, *A Theory of Justice,* 508–9, and is criticized in Louis P. Pojman, "Theories of Equality: A Critical Analysis," *Behavior and Philosophy* 23 (1995): 17–18. If autonomy is a function of (i.e., proportional in some sense to) intelligence, and if the latter property is a matter of degree, the threshold notion of autonomy is probably incorrect. Hence, I have chosen to focus on the more plausible objection that the intrinsic value of persons is an all-or-nothing property.

22. This notion (i.e., the principle of organic unities) comes from G. E. Moore, *Principia Ethica* (Buffalo: Prometheus Books, 1988), 27–29.

23. Noah Lemos provides an argument for the conclusion that the bearers of intrinsic value are facts and states of affairs that obtain. See his *Intrinsic Value* (New York: Cambridge University Press, 1994), 26–31. Unfortunately, Lemos's conclusion is ambiguous. He does not distinguish between the bearer of value being a collection of several things: an actual person, a property, and an instantiation relation between the two, and its being an abstract entity that obtains when all three are present. I will assume but not defend the notion that the bearer of value is the collection rather than the abstract entity.

24. The notion that we can infer moral facts from observations of behavior and belief has come under criticism on the grounds that psychological facts do a better job of explaining these observations, such moral facts would be metaphysically bizarre since they would be intimately linked to human motivation, and the perception of such facts would require a special faculty. Gilbert Harman, *The Nature of Morality: An Introduction to Ethics* (New York: Oxford University Press, 1977), ch. 1; J. L. Mackie, *Ethics: Inventing Right and Wrong* (Middlesex: Penguin Books, 1977), 36–42. My theory works only if these criticisms fail.

25. For a summary of the differences, see Richard Lynn, "Racial and Ethnic Differences in Intelligence in the United States on the Differential Ability Scale," *Personality and Individual Differences* 20 (1996): 271–73. For the case of Asians, see

Richard Lynn, "The Intelligence of Mongoloids: A Psychometric, Evolution, and Neurological Theory," *Personality and Individual Differences* 8 (1997): 813–826. By "Asians" I am referring to the Japanese, Chinese, and Koreans and immigrants from those places. I leave aside the issue whether the pattern repeats itself when other Asian groups are taken into account. For the black-white differences, see Richard J. Herrnstein and Charles Murray, *The Bell Curve,* 276–95 citing *The Testing of Negro Intelligence,* 2d ed., R. T. Osborne and F. C. J. McGurk (Athens: Foundation for Human Understanding, 1982); J. C. Loehlin et al., *Race Differences in Intelligence* (San Francisco: W. H. Freeman and Company, 1975); A. M. Shuey, *The Testing of Negro Intelligence,* 2d ed. (New York: Social Science Press, 1966). Following Michael Levin, I am using race as a stand-in for geographical ancestry plus line (or tree) of descent.

26. An argument for this view can be seen in Howard Gardner, *Frames of Mind: The Theory of Multiple Intelligences* (New York: Basic Books, 1983).

27. Some research has supported that actual genetic differences do exist. See, e.g., Herrnstein and Murray, *The Bell Curve,* ch. 13, although other research finds that non-genetic causes can account for the differences.

My account does not depend on race being a scientifically important category. I do, however, believe that race is a scientifically important category, acting as a stand-in for geographical ancestry, plus line (or tree) of descent. The idea for this point comes from Michael Levin, "The Empirical Reality of Race," unpublished manuscript, 3–4. Thus "white" denotes European antecedents, "black" denotes African antecedents, and "Asian" denotes northeast Asian antecedents. This is not to say that the origin of all human beings is not Africa, but rather that human beings branched into lines that were concentrated in different areas. Nor does the notion that race is a scientifically important category entail that any racial group has a unique genetic factor or factors or a unique phenotypical characteristic or characteristics. This notion also does not entail that intergroup differences are larger than intragroup differences.

28. Michael Levin also concludes that there are per capita racial differences in autonomy. See his *Why Race Matters,* 321–23. Levin argues that this claim receives empirical support from studies indicating the different tendencies of white and black children and adolescents to see what happens to them as a result of uncontrollable external influences rather than their own choices and actions. This tendency is greater in blacks than whites and affects the self-esteem of the white but not black children and adolescents. See ibid. at 322, citing A. Tashakkori, "Race, Gender, and Pre-Adolescent Self-Structure: A Test of Construct-Specificity Hypothesis," *Personality and Individual Differences* 14 (1993): 591–98. Although I think the link between intelligence and autonomy is at least in part conceptual, the empirical evidence may add support to the existence of this link, because it fits nicely with the view that differences in the groups' self-perception are explained in part by reference to metaphysical differences. Levin's moral anti-realism prevents him from drawing any conclusions about the implications of the autonomy-related differences with regard to intrinsic moral value and permissible discrimination (ibid., 213–22).

29. For the overrepresentation of U.S. blacks in crime, see Neil Alan Weiner and Marvin E. Wolfgang, "The Extent and Character of Violent Crime in America, 1969

to 1982," in *Violence*, ed. Neil Alan Weiner et al. (Harcourt Brace Jovanovich, 1990), 32; J. Philippe Rushton, "Race Differences in Behavior: A Review and Evolutionary Analysis," *Personality and Individual Differences* 9 (1988): 1009–24; Michael J. Hindelang, "Race and Involvement in Common Personal Crime," *American Sociological Review* 4 (1978): 93–109.

CHAPTER 7. EXPERIENTIAL DIVERSITY

1. In dissent, Judge Boggs strikingly argued that the court avoided standard procedure, and although he did not explicitly say this, he implied that the avoidance was part of an attempt to gerrymander a particular outcome. In particular, he asserted that Chief Judge Boyce Martin (a Carter appointee) had bypassed the standard random-selection procedure and assigned himself to the three-judge panel that would hear the parties' motions. One of these motions was to temporarily block the lower court's decision against Michigan's program. In addition, the Chief Judge delayed telling the court, which at the time had eleven active members, that the university only petitioned for a full-court review after the two Republican-appointed judges had taken senior status. This prevented the two from participating in the full-court review. A stinging concurrence by Judge Karen Nelson Moore attacked Boggs's procedural argument. She asserted that the Chief Judge's procedure was routine, given the understaffing of the Sixth Circuit and the voluminous number of cases it faced. From the decisions it is impossible to discover who is correct, however, it should be noted that Judge Moore did not dispute the point that the Chief Judge deviated from the court's formal operating procedure.

2. The idea for these three categories comes from George Sher, "Diversity," *Philosophy and Public Affairs* 28 (1999): 98–103.

3. This point comes from Neil Feit.

4. Herrnstein and Murray argue for the existence of such differences in *The Bell Curve*, ch. 13. Their argument has received a lot of criticism. For example, some authors have argued that racial mistreatment and not genetics may account for the data that are used to support the notion of high intraracial heritability of IQ. See Ned Block, "How Heritability Misleads about Race," *Cognition* 56 (1995): 99–128; C. Jencks, *Rethinking Social Policy* (Cambridge: Harvard University Press, 1991), 99, 107; Andrew Hacker, *Two Nations* (New York: Scribner's, 1992), 27. Others object that the inference from genotype to phenotype with a particular IQ that underlies the finding of interracial genetic differences in intelligence is flawed, because the phenotypical patterns may change when we consider unobserved environments. See Block, ibid., figures 4 and 5; D. Layzer, "Science or Superstition: A Physical Scientist Looks at the IQ Controversy," in *The IQ Controversy*, ed. N. Block and G. Dworkin (New York: Pantheon, 1976), 194–241. There are also general objections to the inference from IQ test scores to different genetic aptitudes. A general objection is that there is no such thing as intelligence (as opposed to multiple distinct abilities), and even if there is such a thing as intelligence, it is not measured by IQ tests. In any case, environmental factors alone explain intragroup and intergroup differences. The summary of the different

objections, along with a critical response to them, occurs in Levin, *Why Race Matters,* ch. 3–4, and Max Hocutt and Michael Levin, "The *Bell Curve* Case for Heredity," *Philosophy of the Social Sciences* 29 (1999): 389–415.

5. An extended defense of this claim is provided in Sowell, *Civil Rights: Rhetoric or Reality?*

6. See U.S. Dept. of Commerce, *Statistical Abstract of the United States 2000* (Washington, D.C.: Government Printing Office, 2001), 70.

7. T. Gest, "A Shocking Look at Blacks and Crime," *U.S. News & World Report* (October 16, 1995): 53–54; Hacker, *Two Nations,* 181; N. A. Wiener and M. E. Wolfgang, "The Extent and Character of Violent Crime in America, 1969 to 1982," in *Violence,* ed. Neil Alan Weiner et al. (New York: Harcourt Brace Jovanovich, 1990), 32.

8. The notion that intelligence is to a significant degree heritable is supported by studies that show that identical twins raised in different families have a high degree of similarity in intelligence. These studies suggest that genetic makeup significantly affects intelligence. These studies are summarized in T. J. Bouchard, "The Genetic Architecture of Human Intelligence," in *Biological Approaches to the Study of Human Intelligence,* ed. P. A. Vernon (Norwood, N.J.: Ablex, 1993). There are also adoption studies that indicate that black children have IQ test scores closer to their genetic parents than their adopted white parents, suggesting that the interracial difference in intelligence is in part genetic. See R. Weinberg, S. Scarr, and I. Waldman, "The Minnesota Transracial Adoption Study: A Follow-up of IQ Test Performance at Adolescence," *Intelligence* 16 (1992): 117–35. Herrnstein and Murray estimate that the black-white difference in intelligence is significant (one standard deviation), and that roughly 60 percent of it is hereditary. See Herrnstein and Murray, *The Bell Curve,* 276–80, 298–99.

9. See Herrnstein and Murray, *The Bell Curve,* ch. 5–12.

10. Since these beliefs are favored by the academic left and opposed by the academic right, then one would expect them to be widely held among the heavily left wing faculty in Ivy League and other elite schools. For example, in a poll done by Luntz Research Associates and commissioned by the Center for the Study of Popular Culture, only 6 percent of professors labeled themselves "somewhat conservative," and none labeled themselves "conservative." These percentages fit a similar pattern with party registration and voting. For example in 1995, 3 percent of faculty were registered Republican, whereas 79 percent were registered Democrat. See J. Ryan Gilfoil, "The Review Surveys the Faculty . . . Democrats Dominate," *The Dartmouth Review* 16:5 (1995): 8–9. Similarly, at Brown University, 94.7 percent of the professors with party affiliations were Democrats and 5.3 percent were Republicans. See David Horowitz, "Missing Diversity," *FrontpageMagazine.com,* June 17, 2002.

11. One such broad-based argument is found in William G. Bowen and Derek Bok, *The Shape of the River* (Princeton: Princeton University Press, 1998).

12. The notion of a claim to equal consideration comes from Judith Jarvis Thomson, "Preferential Hiring," in *Equality and Preferential Treatment,* ed. Marshal Cohen

et al. (Princeton: Princeton University Press, 1977), 31–34. The notion that the claim rests on the general demand of justice is found in Lisa H. Newton, "Reverse Discrimination As Unjustified," in *Moral Issues,* ed. Jan Narveson (New York: Oxford University Press, 1983), 388–92. The notion that the claim rests on the greater claim about the white applicant's greater educational interest is defended in Kershnar, "Strong Affirmative Action Programs at State Educational Institutions Cannot Be Justified via Compensatory Justice," 347–50. The notion that the white applicant's claim rests on greater desert is defended in two ways. On one account, the applicant's greater desert rests on his being the best qualified. See Sher, "Qualifications, Fairness, and Desert," 113–27. On a second account, his greater desert rests on having, on average, worked harder than his competitor. See Kershnar, "Strong Affirmative Action Programs," 345–63.

13. These effects are mentioned in Sher, "Diversity," *Philosophy and Public Affairs* 28 (1999): 87. The point about stigmatization comes from Charles Murray, "Affirmative Racism," in *Social Ethics* 4th ed., ed. Thomas A. Mappes and Jane S. Zembaty (New York: McGraw-Hill, 1992), 325–33. The increased failure can be seen in the following sort of results. For persons who started college in the 1992–93 academic year, the dropout rate for blacks at elite colleges was more than twice that of whites, and almost three times more at some of these colleges (e.g., Pennsylvania, Duke, Dartmouth, and Stanford). See ibid. at 408, citing Theodore Cross, "What if There Was No Affirmative Action in College Admissions? A Further Refinement of Our Earlier Calculations," *Journal of Blacks in Higher Education* 5 (Autumn 1994): 55. The balkanization is a worldwide phenomenon as groups compete for political favors. See Sowell, *Race and Culture,* 141–45.

14. In *Grutter,* both the majority and minority got into a broad-scale discussion of the educational benefits of diversity, as shown by an empirical study done on behalf of the University of Michigan. If a discussion of broader social and economic benefits is not relevant, then it is hard to see how the narrower one could be.

15. The idea for this analysis of equality of opportunity comes in part from Michael Levin, "Equality of Opportunity," in *Readings in Social and Political Philosophy,* ed. Robert M. Stewart (New York: Oxford University Press, 1986), 270–81.

16. This concern is nicely set out in James Fishkin, *Justice, Equal Opportunity, and the Family* (New Haven: Yale University Press, 1983), ch. 1–2.

17. The value of the desert-well-being correlation is set out in Shelly Kagan, "Equality and Desert," in *What Do We Deserve?,* ed. Louis P. Pojman and Owen McLeod (New York: Oxford University Press, 1999), 298–314. The value of the no-pattern correlation is defended in Nozick, *Anarchy, State, and Utopia,* 235–38.

Index

affirmative action, 3–5, 33–65, 97–98, 119–29
  private affirmative action, 5, 53–65
  state affirmative action, 4–5, 33–51
  strong affirmative action, 3–5, 33–65
autonomy, 99–109
  capacity, 99–102
  coherentism, 100–1
  condition, 101–2
  higher-order desires, 99–100
  infinite regress of desires, 100
  relation to intelligence, 105–6

Bakke, Regents of California v. (1978), 120–22
Bollinger, Grutter v. (2002), 120–22
Boxill, Bernard, 6, 80

civil rights, 12–13
  bona fide occupational qualification, 12–13, 132–33 n. 6
  Diaz v. Pan American, 13
  PGA Tour, Inc. v. Martin, 13
Coleman, Jules, 56–58, 147 n. 7
compensatory justice, 35–37, 55–58, 71

Diaz v. Pan American, 13
diversity:
  general approach, 126–27
  Grutter v. Bollinger (2002), 120–22
  Regents of California v. Bakke (1978), 120–22
  relation to truth, 122–26

D'Souza, Dinesh, 71
Dworkin, Ronald, 149 n. 5

Epstein, Richard, 134 n. 19
equal opportunity, 128–29

Grutter v. Bollinger (2002), 120–22

harm, 41, 70–71
  causal test, 41
  counterfactual test, 71
  token harm, 41
Herrnstein, Richard, 98–99, 146 n. 1, 147 n. 4, 150 n. 10, 152 n. 27, 153 n. 4, 154 n. 8

intrinsic moral value, 107–9, 151 n. 23
  definition, 107–9
  duties generated by, 111–12
  grounds, 103–5
  threshold theory of, 107–8

job qualification, 11–30
  capacity versus potentiality, 15–16
  concept, 14
  conception, 14–22
  duty to hire according to, 22–26
  employer-centered conception, 19–22

Levin, Michael, 86–87, 147 n. 10, 152 n. 27, 152 n. 28, 153–54 n. 4

Martin, PGA Tour, Inc. v., 13
Meritocracy, 26–27

Murray, Charles, 98–99, 146 n. 1, 147 n. 4, 150 n. 10, 152 n. 27, 153 n. 4, 154 n. 8

Pan American, Diaz v., 13
PGA Tour, Inc. v. Martin, 13
personal identity, 58–59, 73–74
  essential conditions, 74
Pojman, Louis P., 135 n. 30
property rights, 85

Regents of California v. Bakke (1978), 120–22
reparations for slavery, 69–91
  amount, 80–81
  division of claim, 83
  epistemic objections, 84–86
  federal government, 88–89
  inheritance-based model, 76–82
  metaphysical concerns, 83
  offsets, 86–87
  state governments, 89–90
  trustee model, 77–79
right action, 53–54
  correct moral reasoning, 53
  hypothetical imperatives, 53–54
rights, 49, 112–13
  relation to intrinsic value, 112–13

Schedler, George, 88–89, 146 n. 29, 147 n. 8, 148 n. 15
Sher, George, 122, 135 n. 28, 141 n. 9, 141 n. 10
slavery. *See* reparations for slavery
state educational institutions, 33–51

Thomson, Judith Jarvis, 47–50

waiver of rights, 43–50
  culpable wrongdoing, 43–44
  innocent beneficiary, 44–47
  relation to community debt, 47–50

www.ingramcontent.com/pod-product-compliance
Lightning Source LLC
LaVergne TN
LVHW040157080826
844660LV00001B/7
* 9 7 8 0 7 9 1 4 6 0 7 1 9 *